PHARAOH OBAMA I:

The Christian's Response to Tyranny

Dr. Marvin Sprouse, Jr. PhD.

CONTENTS

DEDICATION

This Book is dedicated to the small group of Americans who realize that America is perilously close to being spiritually dismantled, but still cling tightly to the notion that sanity can be restored, and we can possibly become one Nation, America Under God, Again.

QUICK SUMMARY

I have an old friend who was a Chief Master Sergeant in the Air Force. When he was really frustrated he would say, "That really frosts my shorts." There is no direct translation of that expression but it means something like, "Why on earth would anyone do anything as world-class stupid as that." Here is something that puts a heavy coat of frost on my shorts; writers who write for fifty pages and don't tell me the purpose of their book.

Here is my quick summary, right here, before you ever see Chapter One. I want you to read what this book is about and why I spent a few thousand hours writing it. This is not another political analysis book, such as I have already written (THE TRASHING OF AMERICA; How Marxist Thugs Hijacked our Nation,) that book tells about the despicable deeds of a few million cowardly America-haters and God-haters who have turned this magnificent flagship among Nations into a Godless, sniveling excuse for a Nation! Those books typically end with vigorous flag-waving, urging citizens to get politically active and to try and save America, to get this train back on the tracks she once rode with such majesty. Nope, not one of those, because this old man believes America has passed the time when a Political Solution to our many problems still exists. I believe in my heart that no man, no political candidate could right the plethora of wrongs the current renegade government has brought down on us. If we could somehow miraculously recruit a George Washington, an Abe Lincoln or a Ronald Reagan, I doubt that any of those wonder-workers could fix this mess.

Although this is not a political book, politics is, of necessity, part of this story. The engine that drives this book is not about getting out the vote, but it is a communication about you, your spirit, not the spirit of the people, but your spirit, about whether you have already become one of the spiritually walking dead, or whether you are a magnificent success, a soul only waiting to be lifted up to spend forever with your best friend and your personal Savior. Jesus Christ.

The title suggests that President Barack Hussein Obama is our first American Pharaoh. That idea requires a great shift in thinking for my readers, who are almost certainly 99.9% Christian Conservatives. To understand the message of this book you will need to wrap your mind around the theological concept of Divine Reprobation, the fact that God is in charge, and that the world does not turn and respond to anything from any secret society, royal family, august political group or what some man or woman speaks into a microphone on National Radio or TV. It's not about any of that, reader. Everything that happens every day to every one of us is orchestrated by what the Bible refers to as "His good Pleasure," the indisputable will of God. God is large and in charge, and that includes His sovereignty over the fact that our Citizenry, not once, but twice, elected Barrack Hussein Obama as our President. Think for a few seconds about what that means. It means, because God allowed Obama to become what I call the First American Pharaoh, that Pharaoh Obama I is a manifestation of God's Holy and indomitable will.

It is not even possible that a great plague of stupidity infected millions of Americans just before they voted. This author believes that the improbability of Americans electing Barack Obama is so huge that only an act of God could have caused so many people to think so stupidly and vote for a man who has demonstrated to all that he is a human wrecking ball to the American economy and a Chicago thug of a man, acting in the wanton abuse of constitutional power. The Bible shows us that God is capable of bringing strong delusion to wicked people.

II Thessalonians 2:11-12 says, "And for this cause I will send them strong delusion, that they should believe a lie, that they might all be damned who believed not the truth, but had pleasure in unrighteousness." In short the premise of this Book includes the idea that Obama is God's man, bringing to America exactly what we deserve, a severe punishment, which will ultimately include the trashing of nearly all of the precious freedoms we Americans have fought so long and with such profound passion to acquire.

The Bible instructs us that God is slow to anger. That same Bible also teaches that those kind, nurturing hands of God can, in an instant, be transformed into fists. Open hands are designed to love, comfort and help, while fists have a singular and frightening purpose of smashing and delivering harm. How on earth can a Nation go for decades murdering over a million infants every year for the convenience of abortion, and elevate and publically celebrate the sin of homosexuality, clearly described as an abomination in Romans, Chapter One, and turn our backs on God's Chosen people, Israel, without seeing those hands of God come crashing down as wrath-driven fists? In other words just take a look at America and what we are doing and at what we have become. Simply watch television for a night and decide if what you saw will please or anger God.

God used some of the most wicked men in history to execute exactly what He had already planned, way back in time, before Adam ever chomped down on a piece of fruit hanging from a forbidden tree. He used Pharaoh to demonstrate, with that incident at the Red Sea, just how powerful He was. That Red Sea thing was contrived by God, step by step, to bring His people into a trap just so He could demonstrate how He could and would rescue them.

In Romans 9:17, God specifies how he planned to use Pharaoh, "…Even for this same purpose have I raised them up, that I may show my power in you, and that my name may be proclaimed in all the earth." God spoke of a King named Nebuchadnezzar, who had taken His chosen People Israel into total submission, by either executing them or marching them away chained as slaves, as, "my servant, Nebuchadnezzar."

Why would God call the man who enslaved His people, "My Servant?" Nebuchadnezzar was God's servant because he was executing a plan he believed was his own plan, but actually was all about the sovereign will of God. The sovereignty of God is so powerful, that God even controls the moves of Satan, and I'll soon show you how that was so clearly demonstrated in the Book of Job.

Now, move quickly forward from those ancient days

of the Old Testament, to modern times, specifically to 2012. Barack Obama had engineered a public trashing of our economy, running up more debt that every President before him in 53 terms of Office, and tarnished our reputation, traveling early in his Presidency to France, where American service-men had almost single handedly determined that the French people would continue to speak and to be French instead of speaking and becoming German.

Our President went to the very people we liberated and he apologized for American "arrogance", as if we had been conducting long-running bombing raids on Paris. He has bowed to Muslim potentates, and publicly demonstrated his disdain for our Constitution. Then an amazing thing happened. Weeks after the most shameful betrayal imaginable of professional Americans abroad, in the abandonment of our responsibility to our own people in Benghazi, our masses of non-thinking citizens elected him for a second term.

It was the day of Barack Obama's second election that I promised myself and my wife, that I would never become involved in politics ever again. I was not going on the radio to talk about it, or write about it. It was too bizarre and just too stupid to bother with, so I swore off the whole mess.

A wise man once told me to "Never underestimate the power of stupid people in large numbers." That is certainly wisdom if I have ever heard it, but does it extend to electing the most dangerous and unpredictable (as in loose cannon) President ever to serve in the White House? Evidently it does, because only a dunderhead with no appreciation or understanding of how Americans have shed precious blood all over the globe for remarkable freedoms would ever vote for an Obama!

We fought and many died because our hunger for freedom was insatiable enough to drive us to take a rag tag Army of Colonials and kick the daylights out of the allegedly invincible British Nation. We rescued Europe and Asia from Hitler and the Japanese Emperor because it was, simply, the right thing to do.

A few weeks after the 2012 election I heard Rush Limbaugh ask and answer his own question. He said something like this, "People are asking me what should I or could I do now. The Liberal Democrats have taken over our Country, so what is left to say about the Government? My purpose is this ladies and gentlemen. My singular purpose is to make fun of them (Liberals.) Making fun of these people is what they deserve and it serves the purpose of this program, exposing the lunacy of what they do from day to day."

I decided if Rush Limbaugh was announcing that he was going to dedicate his life to making fun of the people who had trashed our Nation, I did not want to listen to Conservative drivel on the air or participate in making jokes about the human wrecking balls of liberal Democrats or turn-coat Republicans, a godless gang referred to by Ann Coulter in her accurate Book, DEMONIC. I decided it was time to stop complaining and find a more noble way to invest whatever precious time this old man has left on Planet Earth.

Read the title of this Book, then take that title at face value and you will declare that I have abandoned my own best intentions. The title surely sounds as if this is just another Political Journal of anger, hatred and meaningless griping. Again, I promise; this is not a political book. It is a Book about God, about you and about your soul. Of necessity I must spend enough ink here to convince you of two things; That America deserves a severe punishment from God, and secondly, that the punishment is happening every time Pharaoh Obama takes another swing at the core freedoms that once made this Nation a great America under God.

I am about to ask a lot of you. I ask you to briefly consider that I am right, and that America is, right this minute, under the harsh judgment and severe punishment of God. Then I am going to ask you to spiritually step back from the vicious debate over whether Liberalism or Conservatism is just, and can save America, and which of those camps is straight out of Hell and fashioned to destroy our Nation?

This one sentence from Rush Limbaugh might help you to breathe a bit of fresh air and realize how fruitless all of this squabbling is. About 20 years ago Mr. Limbaugh was interviewed in TALKERS, a Magazine published by the National Association of Radio Talk Show Hosts of America (NARTSH.) Rush Limbaugh was asked to identify the purpose of his radio program. He responded with something like this.

"There are three purposes for my program: entertainment, entertainment and entertainment." Limbaugh knows what he is doing, and he fully understands the power he holds because "conversationalists across the fruited plain," religiously tune in each day to be entertained, to be entertained and to be entertained. I am suggesting that, just for a brief respite, you back away from your daily dose of conservative talk entertainment, of making fun of the godless mob, which would destroy us all, and examine something more profoundly important and relevant to you and to your eternity.

Take a look not at who is sitting in which Washington Office, but at who/what the driving force is in your life. Are you smirking and spouting off clichés about the ruling czars and clowns of Liberalism, or are you focused on who is the real Supreme Power in Your Life? Are you going to spend eternity being tormented in Hell (Because many of us are definitely marching off in that direction,) or are you a chosen son or daughter of the Risen Lord, bound for Glory, regardless of which liar is elected to which office. All that is happening today tells me that the end is near, very near, that judgment will happen very soon and very suddenly and my sole mission is to be ready for that day of the Lord, and to influence as many as I possibly can to prepare for that day of the Lord along with me.

As previously stated several times, this is not a political book. Neither you nor I have time for the entertainment of yet another election cycle. Who is going to be drafted by which team, or elected to which office, or rewarded because his supporters spent the most money, is not going to influence the Great Judge waiting to see us very shortly. In the great scheme of things only one thing matters, and your clue is that the only thing that matters has nothing to do with any achievement you craft to impress other men.

Pharaoh Obama I is determined to destroy the America our patriots have built, and replace it with a Marxist land of chaos, want and godless depravity. Marxism is not however our greatest threat. The cobra in your sleeping bag is not related to the external events perpetrated by minions of a government most of us will never meet, but to the corruption of our culture, the stage four cancerous decay of our morality, the horrible future of our very souls.

Certainly this sounds crazy to most of you. Before you throw this Book away and warn your friends to avoid me and all that I am communicating, I plead with you to consider this single question, "What if I'm right?" What if political activism and voting is still important, but the main thing is not who we elect but Who we select to follow. I am borrowing this quotation from an unknown preacher who told his congregation, "We don't need more men to pledge allegiance to a Democratic Donkey. We don't need more men to get behind the Republican elephant. What our Nation must have to survive is millions of men, women and children making rock-solid commitments to serve the Lion of Judah."

The last three chapters of this book are most assuredly the most important words of this communication. All that is written before those final three Chapters prepares you, the reader, to understand, to wrap your mind around the message of those final chapters, to follow just a little less what the Liberals are doing to loot and pillage our Nation, and focus on What God can and will do to straighten this mess out so that we Americans do have a future.

Thank you for picking up this book. Read, and be brought closer to God, the only solution to the many huge problems of this Country. The author's core intention is that when you finish reading this Book you will be able to pray, "God Bless America, again" and that you will know exactly what that means.

CHAPTER ONE

The Gradual Emergence of Evil in America

"The Problem with socialism is that you eventually run out of other people's money." **Margaret Thatcher**

THE MESSAGE

Here I sit, back straight, fingers poised above a keyboard, ready to write the most important words of my life, after publishing 25 books which ran from espionage fiction to Bible commentary, with a few self-help and political analysis books sprinkled into the lot. I'm 73 and the world I see depicted by what is often called the main stream media, Hollywood and these stupid idiot boxes we call our TVs (Print media is not worth mentioning in this barely literate culture) is nothing I ever envisioned, contributed to or wanted.

America today, to old fogies such as I, is an assault on the spirit, a nasty intrusion on what was, once upon a time, a pretty good thing, a real-deal America the Beautiful, "My Country Tis of thee" and "The Land of the Free and the Home of the Brave," peopled by God-fearing folk living out lives amid our "amber ways of grain."   Don't let me startle you, America, but some rowdy thugs have invaded our fruited plains and fouled and ruined us and our culture! They crept in with their New American Order, smoking pot they are buying from their own pharmacists, trashing our beautiful language with their BFFs and their OMGs, blurring the clearly defined lines between sexes, transforming thugs to heroes, wrong to right, bad to good, evil to sacred, and they alone are still able to LOL.

America, if you want a genuine and real-deal state of the Union briefing, try these verses from II Timothy Chapter 3. They seem to say all that needs to be said about America today. Begin with verses 1-5, "This know also, that in the last days perilous times shall come. For men shall be lovers of their own selves, covetous, boasters, proud, blasphemers, disobedient to parents, unthankful, unholy, without natural affections, truce breakers, false accusers, incontinent, fierce, despisers of those that are good, traitors, heady, high minded, lovers of pleasure more than lovers of God, having a form of godliness but denying the power thereof; from such turn away,"

Then in the same Chapter, verses 12-13. "Yeah, and all that live godly in Christ Jesus shall suffer persecution, But evil men and seducing shall wax worse and worse. Deceiving and being deceived."

If you dare to read on you will be insulted because I am going to tell you what anyone with those old coke-bottle glasses can see clearly. Anyone with a smear of intelligence can observe enough to know we are now a wicked, dishonest and immoral country peopled primarily by those who would not work if they could, because they believe they are "entitled" to do nothing and receive compensation for their contributions of taking up space, burning oxygen and squandering our resources.

Nobody could ever say we weren't warned. We weren't paying attention when Pharaoh Obama I wrote, in his own words, of his mysterious college days, *"To avoid being mistaken for such a sell-out I chose my friends carefully, the more politically active black students, the foreign students, the Chicanos. The Marxist Professors, the structural feminists and punk-rock performance poets..."* I can imagine what a brilliant intellectual such as Barry Obama (He called himself Barry Sotero back in those days) would have thought of yours truly in the 60s. I was just a little proud to be called a "redneck" and I was usually situated within reaching distance of my rod and reel, I was passionately in love with the game of football and preferred hanging with the R.O.T.C. guys who were called "Gung-Ho," and couldn't wait to get to Viet Nam. We thought that if life was really good to us we could pick up a Ranger Tab and a set of Airborne Wings before they shipped us off to Southeast Asia. Ouhhh Auhhh!

To my crowd, Marxist Professors were some kind of low-life-scum-suckers, true bottom-feeders. only tolerated "up-north" and not worth a glob of spit on a hot day. Of course my ideas have changed and now I know those guys are more low-life, anti-American, Anti-Christ and seriously dangerous than I ever imagined. As for "punk-rock performers"- which sounds like an oxymoron to me, their company would not appeal at all to a guy like me who thought the biggest con of our times was a scrawny little guy named Bob Dillon who had convinced some weirdoes that he could sing. I still remember clearly where I was and what I was doing the first time I heard Johnny Cash sing, "I WALK THE LINE."

Now I invite you to take a great leap forward to the year 2008. By then I was an old guy who was on the radio and wrote occasional books such as one titled POLITICAL CORRECTNESS EXPOSED; A Piranha in Your Bathtub and my more recent work, THE TRASHING OF AMERICA; How Marxist Thugs Hijacked America.

In 2008 I was bewildered when the Republican Party, the traditional home of conservatism in America, nominated a grand old military hero and a flaming liberal of a non-thinking politician, John McCain, as their Presidential Candidate. Then I picked up an article written about Alan Keyes, who had just left the Republican Party after decades of service. You might remember Alan Keyes, who showed up ready to participate in a Republican Debate, in

Atlanta, back in 1996, but he was handcuffed and taken into custody by Atlanta Police. The Police drove Mr. Keyes around until the debate ended. They then released him at the TV Station where he had been arrested.

1. Mr. Keyes had come to a debate with something nobody in the planning group of that Republican debate wanted to hear, intelligent discussion. In an article I read about Alan Keyes, President Reagan was quoted as having said, at a fundraiser, when Alan Keyes was running for a seat in the Senate, "I've never known a more stout-hearted defender of a strong America than Alan Keyes."

2. That sentence did it for me and I became an Alan Keyes fan and supporter as I read those words.

During the 2008 Election I served as the Chairman of the Alan Keyes Campaign in Texas. Through an epic struggle with the bureaucracy in Austin, I managed to get Dr. Keyes' name on the Ballot for the Presidential Election in Texas in 2008. What I had not done was to secure a name for his Vice Presidential Running Mate, and so, at the last possible minute, I entered my own Name as the Vice Presidential running mate with Alan Keyes in Texas.

That is the true story of how a guy known locally as "Crazy Marvin" wound up running, (as one of my West Texas Friends declared) *"Marvin was running as the by-God Vice President of the whole danged United States."* Here is a historical fact you can add to your file of useless trivia. On the final day for registering to be on the ballot in Texas, the Republican and the Democratic parties both missed the Texas deadline for registering, for inclusion on the ballot. If I had missed that deadline I would not have been allowed to have my name entered on the ballot in Texas. In a fair and perfect world the Republicans and Democrats would have been ruled ineligible and Alan Keyes would have won the Presidential Election in Texas by unanimous default. That doesn't matter one bit because we do not live in a fair and perfect world.

My friends dwindled as they realized I was very serious about my support for Alan Keyes, and they accused me of wasting my vote. By that time Alan Keyes had been thoroughly demonized by those who control the media in America, and most thought-free-Americans went along with the flow of spiritual sewage we call the news, and accepted the branding of Alan Keyes as an idiot.

I responded by writing a book titled DON'T WASTE YOUR VOTE. I knew that the true American vote-wasters were conservatives who voted for John McCain simply because he called himself a Republican. Imagine America's only conservative party, representing millions of conservative voters, nominating a liberal. Talk about wasting a vote! Some Conservatives can actually read, walk and chew gum simultaneously, and they will not ever vote for a liberal. My Book, DON'T WASTE YOU VOTE was widely read, and both of those guys said it was a pretty good book.

As it always seems to do, time passed. Pharaoh Obama I, proved (the accusations we had made against him), that he was not only incompetent but ineligible (They called us "birthers," laughed most of us into silence, and never responded to our heavily documented accusations.) Then in 2012 I waited to see if the Republicans had just suffered a colossal brain outage of the masses in 2008, or if they had gone on a strict diet of eating stupid pie for every meal.

The "stupids" won out and the Republicans offered America's Conservatives an opportunity to vote for Mitt Romney. Romney was another Liberal who gave name to the term Rino, Republicans in name only.

After backing presidential candidates John McCain and Mitt Romney, the Republican Party is running on an empty tank where leadership is concerned, and there is no longer a true conservative party in this Nation. They (The Republican Leadership) obviously thought leading America was some great TV game show and since the Democrats had been winning elections they would return to power by abandoning the conservative values which had been driving Republicanism, and attempted to make Democrats (Rinos) out of all of us. Thanks, oh great and stupid ones!

If anyone held a tiny glimmer of hope for sanity in 2012, that was destroyed with two actions, the introduction of the great cell phone bribe and the greatest racial atrocity in American History. Just before the election, the Obama Camp reached into a boat load of cell phones and started giving them away. It would be very, very difficult to find one of those cell phones in use today because they came complete with annoyances called monthly bills and things like roaming charges. Thus we have a new truth of American Wisdom; THERE ARE NO FREE CELL PHONES.

That brings us to what will make my name hated by many, throughout the land of the free and the home of the brave. I am going to call the fact that between 93 and 96 % of black Americans voted for Pharaoh Obama what it is, a racial atrocity. People like Colin Powell and JC Watts said they "Had to" vote for Obama because he was black. The day might come America, when over 90% of white Americans just might say something as stupid as, "I just had to vote for Mr. Jones because he is white." Probably not, but can you understand how tacky and racist that is? If not, then God help us all. Why did not a single major newspaper or TV station or so-called-conservative radio talk show host call that 93% figure a racial incident? Why? Why not? Can you, in your wildest dreams imagine George Bush Jr. or Sr. saying something like, "I had to vote for Romney because he was the white guy?" Not in your wildest dreams. It just would not or could not happen!

The most talented man to ever turn on a microphone in Texas is Mark Davis. I heard Mark Davis say something like this about two years ago. He said. (paraphrasing,) "Blacks will vote for a black candidate always and every time. It doesn't matter if he is in jail, or missing, or dead. They will still say 'He's got my back', and they will vote for him." A few days later Mark Davis disappeared from WBAP. Thank goodness, he resurfaced on another Local Dallas Station. I believe that anyone who addresses what Black America perpetrated on themselves and all Americans, is something that desperately needs to be addressed.

So my next question is this, "What's worse, A retired Army General and former Secretary of State announcing that he has to vote for a particular candidate because he is allegedly black, or Paula Dean admitting that she used that horrible "N Word" a few decades ago? I know this and I know it is absolute truth; If some white General had said that he was going to vote for Romney because he was white he would have been destroyed in a matter of hours; destroyed, finished, left in a dark and smoking heap of ash. That isn't right, and racism in America will never be a part of our history until we treat all races, even the hated white race, with equal justice and censure.

To fully appreciate just how catastrophic the 2012 election was, I need to insert a story here about my two Cajun friends, Boudreaux and Tibbedeaux. Old Boudreaux and Tibbedeaux were watching the ten o'clock news one night when the cameras picked up a shot of a woman on the ledge of a high building in downtown Baton Rouge. Tibbedeaux said, "I'll bet you twenty dollars that she gonna jump." Boudreaux said, "I'll take that bet." A few minutes later both men watched as the woman sprang from the ledge in a beautifully executed swan dive. Boudreaux pulled out his wallet, took out a twenty dollar bill and handed it to Tibbedeaux. Then Tibbedeaux said, "I can't take your money. I watched this on the six o'clock news." Boudreaux then said, I saw that too , and I just didn't think she would jump twice."

So help me America, that is the best that I can manage, when it comes to explaining how America elected Pharaoh Obama I, not once but twice. There is just possibly room for comprehension why many blacks, liberals and young and stupid voters did what they did in 2008. They thought, "Hey, it's time for a black guy to be president," or "we've had enough of conservatism and we know that isn't working, so let's try this liberal guy," or "It's true that he has no track record, but maybe that's a good thing and we can get some new ideas in Washington."

Others were thinking that Obama would somehow install a new utopian culture in America, and we could all go in peace and feast on the sweetness of the flow from The Big-Rock-Candy-Mountain. "The Big- Rock-Candy-Mountain," is a phrase from a Harry McClintock song he wrote in the 1920s about how starving millions might conjure up an imaginary solution for their persistent hunger.

3. Peggy Joseph thought that, and believed with all of her heart, that Pharaoh Obama I was going to magically make her wealthy. There is an infamous u-tube video of Miss Joseph, a young Florida woman who skipped school to attend an Obama Rally in 2008. After Peggy Joseph had been inspired by the Pharaoh-in-waiting, she said. ""It was the most memorable time of my life. It was a touching moment. Because I never thought this would happen. I won't have to worry about putting gas in my car. I won't have to worry about paying my mortgage. You know, if I help him, he's gonna help me."

Recently, Joel Gilbert produced a full length documentary titled, "THERE'S NO PLACE LIKE UTOPIA." In that Film Mr. Gilbert found Peggy Joseph, the young lady who passionately believed, in 2008, that President Obama was going to put gas in her car and pay her mortgage) knocked on her door and asked what she thought about President Obama after six years of having him in office. Miss Joseph said, "He (Obama) was not who we thought or expected him to be." Then she said, "Truth and honesty are important. He (Obama) lied about everything."

4. The great tragedy is that Peggy Joseph was no aberration, no attendee from the Central Florida Village Idiot's Convention. No. Peggy Joseph was the face of America's mob of liberal, Democratic voters. Peggy Joseph was the modern version of the Liberal Everyman. Peggy and millions very much like her stood in line to vote, believing the hard times were now history, and Pharaoh Obama I was going to make it all good, like it had never been, and that they would all live at the base of that Big-Rock -Candy-Mountain.

If Peggy Joseph was the face of truth in America, we could ask her who she really is. If young Miss Joseph told Pharaoh with a candidate named Mitt Romney? Compared to the powers that be in the Republican Party, the Peggy Josephs of the world really do appear intelligent.

This story has a very happy ending, Today, Peggy Joseph, is an attractive, working mother, who knows exactly what a liar looks like and she probably won't be fooled by an Obama or anyone like him again. Peggy Joseph is making herself a walking success story, but to achieve that she had to endure the disappointment of learning that she would have to make things happen for herself, and that no smooth-talker from Chicago was going to fulfill her dreams. Way to go, Peggy Joseph!

If I were a traditional author I would now launch out into 20 or 30 pages about the specifics of how Obama proved his incompetence during the first four years of his Pharaoh-ship. I am not traditional, and I proved that by trying to explain the 2012 election by telling you a story about Tibbedoux and Boudreaux. In that spirit, allow me to now tell you why Pharaoh Obama was re-elected in 2012, by addressing one thing about Pharaoh Obama, which can be quantitatively examined, the horrible and juvenile things he did with money, our money, my money and your money!

On January 19, 2013, CNS News.com issued an article with this headline, FIRST TERM, Obama Increased Debt $50,521 Per Household; More Than First 42 Presidents in 53 Terms Combined. 5. How bad can things get? Just keep watching the Pharaoh and you shall see my friend, and it is this humble author's opinion that you "ain't seen nothin' yet!

Now I come to the point about how spiritual thugs respond to the news that they are spending your money as fast as they can print it. They respond by impugning the source. The Obama people, through one of their promotional agencies, The Huffington Post, turned the blame for their financial disaster on the Republicans and said they had been wrongly criticized, and they began calling Republican Candidate Mitt Romney, "Romney the liar." That's it? Is that all they have to do to get around the fact that their fiscal misconduct is sort of like the monkey in a tree with a machine gun. They have had to work very hard to trash our economy as thoroughly as they have managed to do. The True-believers in Pharaoh Obama I simply erase bothersome facts from memory and respond with the chant that Romney is a liar (All Liberal rhetoric seems to be transferable to chants, slogans and small signs they can wave at the CNN and TV Network Cameras.)

Logic and sound reasoning would have convinced an intelligent analyst that Pharaoh Obama I was a non-electable entity. Who after all, would vote for a fiscal hand grenade, a man who clearly established an unbreakable record for wasting our money? The 2012 election had nothing to do with the popularity or support winning attributes of Mitt Romney. It was, to a thinking citizen, all about the Pharaoh and his insanely incompetent mis-management of our money. The Key message in that last sentence was the phrase "thinking citizen." Here is truth, Americans, we live in a non-thinking society. Millions of Americans will totally ignore warning signs of danger and incompetence if they are convinced that they can get a free cell-phone, or some other monetary trinket or benefit.

The election came and the impossible happened. I call that sort of occurrence a miracle. The miracle was that Pharaoh Obama I won the 2012 election.

Let me define miracle. Magic is the happening of something that could not possibly happen. Most of what we call magic is illusion, but some of it might be attributable to demonic powers. Something very different from magic is a miracle. A miracle is an act of God, an event created by God wherein He determines the outcome and allows that to happen, through the good pleasure of His will.

I thought long and hard about the second time Pharaoh I was elected, and decided that as illogical, as downright crazy as that was, it had happened. Then I realized that it could have only happened if God had allowed it to happen. Years ago I abandoned any small belief that America was still a Nation under God. A Nation under God does not murder 1.3 million babies each year, celebrate homosexuality or turn its back on Israel. Face it, readers, America was founded as a Nation under God, but we have become a mob of degenerates, an evil Nation with no significant spiritual anchoring. In struggling to make sense of what had happened during the 2012 election, the Biblical wisdom kept coming back to me. In Proverbs 3:5 we read, "Trust in the Lord with all thine heart, and lean not onto thine own understanding." So our election came and passed in 2012, and nothing in my own understanding prepared me for the result.

Stay with me, please, readers, because this is probably not something you have heard in your church. I have heard it in my Church, because we believe in the absolute sovereignty of God and of His Divine will. Because God is sovereign, the doctrine of Divine Reprobation is solid theology and true. In the next Chapter I will prove that God is indeed sovereign, today and just as He was sovereign in Pharaoh's Day.

For now, allow me to deliver the major premise of this Book. Barack Obama is in The White House because it was God's Holy Will that he be our leader. God's purpose is obviously to punish a sinful Nation. God is certainly slow to anger, but we have exceeded the limit of God's wrath and Barack Hussein Obama is precisely the man God sent to punish America.

SOME MAJOR POINTS OF THIS CHAPTER

1. America is very far removed from being the Nation under God she was when she was founded, and much of the change we have experienced is not good or positive. In the development of spiritual character we have been moving backwards for over 50 years.

2. Churchill could certainly have been talking about America in the 21st Century when he said, "To expose the flaw in a democracy, just talk to an average voter for five minutes."

3. The fact that over 93% of black Americans voted for Obama is proof that racism is a driving force in our electoral process.

4. If an American vote can be bought with a cell phone, then American democracy has no future.

5. In the past two elections conservatism was not represented by either major candidate, and that is a primary reason why Liberals are still in power.

CHAPTER TWO

OBAMA IS GOD'S MAN IN WASHINGTON

"Virtue is persecuted more by the wicked than it is loved by the good." **Buddha**

"To see and listen to the wicked is already the beginning of wickedness." **Confucius**

THE SOVEREIGNTY OF GOD

God is sovereign, and that was clearly demonstrated when God spoke to Moses, telling him exactly what was going to happen in Egypt, and very specifically to Pharaoh.

In Exodus 7:3-5. God speaks to Moses, "And I will harden Pharaoh's heart, and multiply my signs and my wonders in the land of Egypt. But Pharaoh shall not harken unto you that I may lay my hand upon Egypt, and bring forth mine armies, and my people the children of Israel, out of the land of Egypt, by great judgments. And the Egyptians shall know that I am the Lord, when I stretch forth my hand and bring out the children of Israel from among them."

In that verse God describes in detail what He is about to do, and He tells Moses and Aaron that He himself will harden Pharaoh's heart. God hardened the heart of the single man who was responsible for holding His people captive. That does not make sense to us, but then again, if we lean not on our own understanding and look for God's motivation we will find it in Exodus 9:16, when God explains precisely why he is prolonging the agony of Israel's slavery. In this verse God is telling Moses, word for word, what to say before Pharaoh, "And in very deed, for this cause have I raised thee up, for to shew in thee my power; and that my name may be declared throughout all the earth."

God decides what will and what will not happen, right down to the smallest detail. That is what I believe. When man is saved or aided by the grace of

God, regardless of what is happening to him on earth in the carnal sense, we call that God's Sovereign Grace. Many men like to clarify the concept of God's grace claiming that God's grace is responsible for much that happens, but man and his free will is equally important in determining what will happen, when it will happen and how it will happen. Jesus saves, and He alone decides who will be saved. Man's free will comes into play when he either moves to accept or to reject temptation.

Many years ago I listened as a Seminary Professor explained, *"Grace, with anything added to it is no longer grace."* I believe that is an accurate statement. This doctrine is so very clearly detailed in Ephesians Chapter One and any who would refute the truth of Election must begin by refuting Ephesians, Chapter one (Along with dozens of other verses.) Consider Ephesians 1:4-5, *"According as He hath chosen us in Him before the foundation of the world. That we should be holy and without blame before him in love: having predestined us unto the adoption of Children by Jesus Christ to himself, according to the good pleasure of His will."* Then In the Same Chapter, verse 11, it is written, *"In whom also we have obtained an inheritance, being predestined according to the purpose of Him who worketh all things after the counsel of His own will."*

This truth of Sovereign Grace is lumped into a body of fact usually referred to as Calvinism. I don't like being called a Calvinist because John Calvin did not think up the doctrines of Grace, but he merely codified and explained them. I prefer to be called a Sovereign Grace Baptist, and don't like being named after anything Calvin did, because Mr. Calvin was especially hateful toward we Baptists. Probably the most succinct explanation of how salvation works is found in Ephesians 2:8, *"For by grace are ye saved, through faith: and that not of yourselves, it is a gift of God: not of works, lest any man should boast."* Those who oppose the doctrines of Grace are infuriated to be told that they themselves do not "earn" salvation, but passively receive it as a gift from God.

Not long ago, I spent an hour explaining how God's plan for salvation works, and when I finished one lady said, "Okay, but we still have to earn it." Obviously I didn't explain it well enough to change what she had been told for fifty years. Brothers and sisters, we are not worthy of salvation, and we cannot earn it, not ever. We simply are not good enough to earn salvation from the living God! Review the final words of the verse I presented in the previous paragraph, *"..it is a gift of God, not works, lest any man should boast."*

It was a wise man, whose name I don't remember, who wrote, "There is nothing more pitiful on this earth than a man trying to earn his salvation by himself." Here is one more powerful passage on how Jesus and His crucifixion saved us. John 10:27-30 instructs us, *"My sheep hear my voice, and I know them, and they follow me: And I give unto them eternal life, and they shall never perish, neither shall any man pluck them out of my hand. My Father, which gave them me, is greater than all, and no man is able to pluck them out of my Father's hand. I and my Father are one."*

God uses each of us, even the most wicked of us to fulfill His Holy Will. Pharaoh was one hard headed man, and when God began to shower curse after curse on Egypt, Pharaoh should have broken down and given in much sooner than he did. When Moses put forth his staff and the waters of Egypt turned to blood, that would have and should have been all that was needed for Pharaoh, or any other ruler. It was not, and who was directing Pharaoh's behavior? None other than the living God of the Israelites. Of course, Pharaoh thought he was the brave and fearless leader who was not afraid of the horrible things Moses had brought on the Egyptians. Surely in his heart, he was thinking, "I'll show the God of the Israelites. He doesn't know who He is dealing with here. I am Pharaoh and I myself am a god! We'll just see who is the strongest god in this little drama."

Then, When Pharaoh did indeed harden his own heart, thinking it was of his own strong and fearless will, it was a hardening that God had already promised Moses was going to occur. In Exodus 4:21 we find an account of God talking to Moses, *"And the Lord said unto Moses, When thou goest to return into Egypt, see that thou does all those wonders before Pharaoh, which I have put into thy hand: but I will harden his heart, that he shall not let the people go."* Then, in Exodus 7:13 we read, *"And He (God) hardened Pharaoh's heart."*

Man believes he controls his own destiny and he loves to think and say things such as that. He does not control anything, but God is touching everything that happens or fails to happen. To illustrate how total God's will is in the operation of the Universe visit the First Chapter of the Book of Job.

In Job 1:6, we read of a meeting in heaven, presided over by God and attended by none other than Satan. Job 1:6 instructs us, *"Now there was a day when the Sons of God came to present themselves before the Lord, and Satan came also among them. And the Lord said unto Satan, Whence comest thou? Then Satan answered the Lord, and said, From going to and fro in the earth, and from walking up and down in it."* Satan described, with those words, a disciplined route he had been walking, indicating that he had been conducting military patrols. In I Peter, 5:8, Peter clarifies what those patrols of Satan's were all about, *"Be sober, be vigilant, for your adversary the devil, as a roaring lion, walketh about, seeking whom he may devour."* When Satan told God that he had been walking about on the earth, God knew that He (Satan) had been seeking the destruction of souls (vulnerable souls to "devour.")

This next verse seems strange to a believer who does not know the ways of God. *"And the Lord said unto Satan, hast thou not considered my servant Job, that there is none like him in the earth, a perfect and upright man, one that feareth God, and escheweth evil?"*

It appears that God is offering Job up to Satan, selling him out. The truth is that God is working His own plan to have Satan tempt Job for the purpose of making Job even stronger and more righteous. This principle is described in Hebrews 12: 6-8, "For whom the Lord loveth he chasteneth. And scourageth every son whom he receiveth. If ye endure chastening, God dealeth with you as sons, for what son is he whom the Lord chasteneth not? But if ye be without chastisement, whereof all are partakers, then are ye bastards and not sons." The purpose of the chastisement God gives to all whom He loves, is clarified in James 1:2-4, *"My brethren, count it all joy when ye fall into great temptations (tribulations;) knowing this, that the trying of your faith worketh patience. But let patience have her perfect work, that ye may be perfect and entire, wanting nothing."*

When God suggests that Satan, "consider my servant Job," He is preparing to chastise Job, thereby strengthening him. Note how God always maintains absolute control over all that happens, even the releasing of Satan. In Job 1:12, God gives permission to Satan to attack Job, but He specifies the limitations of the pain Satan may inflict, *"And the Lord said unto Satan, Behold, all that he (Job) hath is in thy power, only upon himself put forth not thine hand..."* God allowed Satan to go and to tempt Job, but even in that situation, God maintained control, instructing Satan not to touch Job physically.

If God controls everything that happens on earth, then how can anyone explain the destruction of the World Trade Center towers on 911? I believe that the 911 attack was succinctly explained by a man who was ridiculed and literally laughed into silence by an American citizenry who could not handle the truth and refused to even consider it.

On September 14th, 2001, three days after the attack on the Twin Towers, Jerry Falwell appeared on Pat Robertson's 700 Club and said, "What we saw on Tuesday, as terrible as it was, could be miniscule if, in fact, God continues to lift the curtain and allow the enemies of America to give us probably what we deserve."

Pat Robertson added, "Well, Jerry, that's my feeling." A few days later, after a veritable fire storm of criticism was fired off at Falwell and Robertson, Falwell issued what was not much of an apology at all, while Robertson posted on his website an apology, blaming Falwell for inappropriate comments and for getting out of control.

Falwell continued, "The ACLU has got to take a lot of blame for this. And I know I'll hear from them for this. But throwing God...successfully with the help of the federal court system...throwing God out of the public square, out of the schools, the abortionists have got to bear some of the burden for this because God will not be mocked and when we destroy 40 million little innocent babies, we make God mad...I really believe that the pagans and the abortionists and the feminists and the gays and the lesbians who are actively trying to make that an alternative lifestyle, the ACLU, People for the American Way, all of them who try to secularize America...I point the finger in their face and say you helped this happen."

It would be so easy, so effortless to join the mainstream media and the dozens of radical left wing, politically correct, belly-achers and blame Falwell and Robertson, and many other nationally known evangelists for bashing the left wing activists, but there were a handful of men and women, who looked at America, who listened to Falwell and concluded that if God is Sovereign, even though He is slow to anger, He will also, as Jerry Fallwell said, not be mocked. How can we murder 1.3 million babies a year, (Woops, my editor just told me that the number of annual abortions in America is now 1.6 million!) celebrate the sin of homosexuality God condemned, and repeatedly turn our back on Israel, and not see the fist of God? How could God not have been instrumental in 911?

THE IMPORTANT POINTS IN THIS CHAPTER

1.   In ancient Egypt God controlled Pharaoh, even the dictator's deepest and most closely held thoughts. In Exodus 7:35 God told Moses, "I will harden Pharaoh's heart."

2.   God sometimes uses evil men to perform His will.

3.   Because of his ego, man likes to think that he engineered his own salvation, having "made a decision" for Christ. In fact, God always makes the decision and man simply receives salvation.

4.   In Job 1, we read that God even controls Satan.

5.   I agree with Jerry Falwell who said that the attack on 911 was God's response to evil in America. Falwell's statement was a truth most Americans refused to even consider.

CHAPTER THREE
LIBERAL DEMOCRATS; THE
AUDACITY OF EVIL

"When I despair I remember that all through history, the way of truth and love have always won. There have been tyrants and murderers, and for a time, they can seem invincible, but in the end they always fail. Think of it-always." **Gandhi**

"People who claim that they are evil are usually no worse than the rest of us...It's people who claim that they're good, or any better than the rest of us, that you have to be wary of. **Gregory Margulie, THE LIFE AND TIMES OF THE WICKED WITCH OF THE WEST.**

"Evil isn't the real threat to the world. Stupid is just as destructive as evil, maybe more so, and it's a hell of a lot more common. What we really need is a crusade against stupid." **Jim Butcher, Vignette**

GOD-HATING INSTITUTIONALIZED BY THE DEMOCRATIC PARTY

Calling people names such as stupid or evil is not on a high level in terms of human communication. Everything I am about to write about how lacking in integrity and hateful of God and of His creations (including mankind) Liberals have become, something similar about me and my people (Christian Conservatives) can and will be said.

The fact is that it is so remarkably easy to demonstrate Liberal misbehavior because it occurs so frequently. The misbehaving Liberals are spiritually immunized against ideals such as human decency and even the most fundamental codes of conduct. It is their Machiavellian immunity to such things as morality and principals that prompts them to lie with unabashed abandon and to behave as if they were gods and had authored all the commandments they need or respect.

All people harbor the potential for terrible behavior, but Liberals celebrate socially abhorrent and culturally destructive misbehavior (such as living out your perceived "right" to abstain from work and live off of Government's so-called entitlements, to rewrite the definition of a marriage and of a family by elevating homosexuals to the status of parents they could never achieve normally, your hatred of God and of America, etc., etc.) with such passion because they actually have lost contact with the concepts of right and wrong. Michel Savage summed it all up succinctly in the title of his bestselling Book, *"LIBERALISM IS A MENTAL DISORDER."*

About 20 years ago I was doing research for a book on political correctness in the main Library in Las

Cruces, New Mexico. I used the big Library edition of Webster's and looked up the word, "liberal." It was a massive book and probably weighed over 20 pounds. When I found the listing for liberal it was about 800 words defining the term. I remember one phrase that sort of jumped out at me, and seemed to capture the core spirit of liberalism. The term was , "lacking in moral restraint."

Liberals hate being told what they can and cannot do. One woman posted a website asking people to come to a retreat she operated. She wrote, that she wasn't into "all of those religious 'thou-shalt-nots." Christianity is filled with thou-shalt-nots, and I am grateful for those explanations of what behaviors God has commanded me to avoid. I have played football and basketball and one thing I respect are the clearly defined boundaries of those games. You will find what is the most famous "thou-shalt-not" in all of history where God told Adam and Eve, in Genesis, Chapter 2:16-17, "...of every tree of the garden thou mayest eat, But of the tree of the knowledge of god and evil, thou shalt not eat of it; for in the day that thou eatest thereof thou shalt die."

Most of us, we conservatives, love and embrace those thou-shalt-nots, for it is the commandments to abstain that provide boundaries for life. Life with clearly defined and respected boundaries provides a high sense of order and of some predictability. Life without boundaries results in chaos, and as I will soon explain "chaos," is highly exalted by liberals. They love chaos, and actually believe that order "evolves" from chaos.

LIBERALS AND INTEGRITY-FREE LIVING

One thing highly prized by conservatives and

passionately hated by liberals is truth. Conservatives reason that only when something is true does it have any legitimate value and is worth following. Liberals, on the other hand often despise truth and see it only as an effort, invented by conservatives, to spoil their lives, by limiting their behavior. Because Liberals are lacking in self-restraint, they view truth as the vampire understands the light of morning, an intrusion designed to destroy their lives. Truth defines acceptable behavior and therefore limits what man does. Chaos, on the other hand, has no absolute truth, and leaves man to do whatever he wants to do, to whomever he wants to do it, whenever he pleases. The old saying we saw on bumper stickers in the 60's, "If it feels good do it" is at much of a core value to liberals as "Love thy neighbor" is to Christians.

Twenty five years ago a lady told me of an incident that had occurred at The Turner Network Headquarters in Atlanta. Ted Turner had just walked out of a studio where his people had put the finishing touches on a documentary they had produced on Russia. Mr. Turner was complimenting the work on the documentary and he asked employees standing around him for their opinions. One lady courageously ventured, "But it's not true." Ted Turned glared at the woman and snapped, "What's that got to do with anything?" Seeking truth on a major TV Network is like a dying man trying to conjure up water by rubbing grains of sand together.

I was driving across Texas one day during 2008 and as I drove, and drove and drove, I listened to talk radio. Every commentator was talking about the debate between Candidate Obama and Candidate McCain, which had been held the previous night. It was a grand mish-mash, a very long and absolutely senseless game of 'He said and he said, and he meant and he meant, and he didn't say this and he didn't say that.' For some reason I cannot explain I finally got home and turned on my TV for just a little bit more of the dribble of nonsense. It had been like listening all day to the Mad-Hatter talking to Peter Rabbit. Then Lou Dodds came on my TV screen and captured the essence of the thousands of words I had heard that day, when he said, simply, "They're both lying." It was at that moment that I swore off listening to the malarkey-driven debates for the remainder of the Political Season. If all you hear are lies what is the point in listening? The answer to that question is obviously, "No point at all."

During those days back in 2008 I was still believing a man, a good man, the right man, could and would be able to straighten out the mess men had made of American Politics. I had found only one man who made the kind of sense I needed to hear. That man was Ambassador Alan Keyes, a man who had been portrayed by the mainstream press as a Jesus-Freak, a fool and a zealot. Dr. Keyes was available to talk to, on teleconferences held a couple of times each week. One evening a woman on one of those conferences summed up why Dr. Keyes was such a viable Presidential Candidate. She said, "I heard you speak 20 years ago, and then I heard you speak again last week. The things you said at each of those events has not changed. You obviously are not trying to keep up with what is popular and what people think they want to hear. You just tell your truth and that is so very refreshing to me."

During those days I often heard Alan Keyes talk about how he favored principles over politics. Ladies and gentlemen this author is convinced that there are certain moral absolutes, things which are right and very definitely - things which are wrong! The God-given spiritual rules and commandments are unchangeable, and those commandments preclude such weak and worthless answers to questions about what is right and what is wrong, such as, "it depends." Readers, abortion is an evil form of murder and homosexuality is a sin capable of earning a perpetrator an eternity in Hell.

Forget all of the Politically Correct Droppings of spiritual dung, (Yes that is a biblical term found in the writings of Paul, Philippians 3:8.) which tell you that sin is to be celebrated and that virtue is silliness. God is Sovereign and adherence to His Word is far more important that the rambling silliness of any Supreme Court or self-appointed Washington Potentate. Every one of us will be judged and that judgment will have nothing to do with whether or not our behavior was politically correct. No Commandment of God was ever issued in the form of a suggestion. Right and wrong are real, and they are always, and every time, ordained by God and His Word.

One of the most important timbers in the construction of a well-working and functional society is truth. Without prevailing truth all communication becomes as dung, waste flung into the wind.

I am certainly not going to advance a notion that Liberals have any Corporate monopoly on lying. What I will describe is a culture where Liberal Politicians have assaulted the virtue of truth-telling and have dragged lying, down to new depths of despicable deceit.

DEMOCRATIC PRESIDENTS: 2 WOMANIZERS AND A SODOMIZER

If you want to dig up the stuff for a book on

Pornography, you need look no further than the escapades in misbehavior of the past few Democratic Presidents. Start with President Kennedy. One of his numerous sexual partners, other than his wife, Jackie, was none other than Marilyn Monroe, the very first female to pose nude for the centerfold pages of Playboy Magazine. Miss Monroe died under circumstances that have spurned almost as many conspiracy theories as the assassination of President Kennedy. I believe Miss Monroe sealed her fate the night she sang the most sexually suggestive song I ever heard, and that song was the Happy Birthday Song she sang for and to President Kennedy, at a birthday Party given for him, at Madison Square Garden in 1962.

If you have seen a video of that performance you know why I call it the most sexually suggestive song this old man ever heard. Men who have seen films or videos of that performance have not forgotten what they saw. To any male member of our species that performance is unforgettable. I can see it clearly right now even though it has been over 50 years since I last saw it. My personal conspiracy theory is that the powers that be (behind the Kennedy Cabal) saw that performance, decided it had gone too far in making public fun of the President's extra marital sexual adventures, and decided to subtract the name of Marylyn Monroe from the rolls of the human race. Interestingly she was introduced that night as "The late Marilyn Monroe." The MC was actually referring to her late arrival on the stage, but the referral of the "late Marilyn Monroe, " still appears ominous in light of the fact that she soon died a mysterious death.

I attended the Military Intelligence School in 1968 at Fort Holabird, in Maryland. I heard from several young men who had been friends with other men our age in the Secret Service, and some of those agents and former agents had talked of late night vigils they had spent sitting in cars outside of apartments, homes and condos around Washington D.C. while President Kennedy was having lengthy nocturnal visits with various women.

Bill Clinton brought philandering to a new low-water mark during his presidency. Not only were the ranks of his sexual partners long and extensive, but the adolescent lies he manufactured, while trying to cover the tracks of his pursuits were often comic in their scope and because of their urgent manufacture. His impassioned plea, which was aired on the early National News across America, has become the most famous, or infamous words he spoke during his entire presidency. The President of the United States, Bill Clinton, looked into the lens of a camera and spoke, feigning his own indignant irritation that anyone should dare to question him and said, "I want to say this to the American People. I want you to listen to me. I'm going to say this again. I did not have sexual relations with that woman, Miss Lewinsky. I never told anyone to lie. Not a single time. These allegations are false. I need to get back to work for the American People. Thank you." There was then heard a burst of applause from those in the room, proving that Liberals are not only immoral, but really, really, really gullible.

After President Clinton made his famous statement about how he "did not," he was busted and embarrassed into admitting that he did have oral sex with, "That woman," and then he magnified his offence with a lie that ranks with up there with the "...but, I-didn't-inhale-whopper." He said ,"I didn't know oral sex was sex..." That fabrication at least partially inspired a pandemic of children ages as low as 12 for many girls swapping oral sex for rides to the mall. Imagine you are the father of a daughter and you walk into your living room one night and see your daughter in the act of giving some squirrelly teen oral sex. The question of the moment is, "Is what you are seeing sex?" If you say, "I don't know," or, "Maybe," or "It depends," or even, "No, that's not sex because the President of the United States said it wasn't sex." then you are most assuredly an unfit parent, and belong with the massive group of American Liberals who are immoral and really, really, really gullible.

In a Book she wrote and published Sharlene Azam, a Canadian author, described the effects of the oral sex epidemic in Canada, and most certainly in the United States. Her Book is titled ORAL SEX IS THE NEW GOODNIGHT KISS: The Sexual Bullying Of Girls. In her Book, author Azam describes a scene in an elementary school where students gathered and blocked passage in a hallway. In the middle of their circle twelve year old girls were performing oral sex on boys.

OUR HOMSEXUAL PRESIDENT

The announced purpose of the Presidential trip was to inspect the crises on the Texas Border with hoards of undocumented "children" flooding across our border with Mexico from places like Honduras, El Salvador and Guatemala. Last week I went to the VA Clinic here in Fort Worth to have blood taken. I waited in line holding a number in my hand for two hours, and then was sent to wait in another line for another hour. Veteran friends of mine have died waiting for treatment for the damage done to their bodies by Agent Orange. While visiting my children in Colorado Springs, I went to a building reported to be the site of a new and modern VA Clinic/Hospital. I took a test which categorized me into a list to be given an appointment during the next 30 days. Two years have passed and I have not heard from the VA in Colorado Springs. VA Treatment is a National joke while Obama is engineering things like this carefully planned run on our border. Meanwhile Veterans are hanging around on the National trash heap of treatment. Pharaoh Obama says now that he can solve the problem on our border for a mere 3.7 Billion US Dollars.

An article in the Washington Times, written by Stephan Dinan and published on July 8, 2014, details how President Obama wants to spend $3.7 Billion US Dollars dealing with the crises he and his people engineered by encouraging illegals, most of them children, to flood the southern borders of the United States. Don't think for a minute that money is intended to be used to feed, clothe and house those illegal immigrants. A whopping amount of those funds are already intended to pay for more judges to adjudicate cases and to be used as "aid" in Central American Countries.

When Obama was in Texas he received repeated and urgently communicated requests, from both Republican and Democratic leaders to come south and see the problems on the Texas-Mexico Border. The President, as he has done so often during the past six plus years simply ignored the requests and made no response. Instead of investigating the real problems of the flood of unwanted illegals swarming into Texas, he went to lunch, cutting to the head of a very long line at the locally famous Franklin Barbeque. When the Cashier, a local entertainer and part-time employee of the Restaurant, Donald Rugg Webb, Saw President Obama he slammed his hands down on the counter and shouted, "Equal Rights for gay people." Obama smiled broadly and asked, "Are you gay?" and the cashier answered, "Only when I have sex." Obama laughed and said , "Bump me, " as he extended his fist to Webb. I am insulted by a photo of my Fist-Bumping President which was published in the July 13, 2014 issue of The Daily Dot, in an article written by Sarah Weber. The article was titled "Obama Austin barbeque fist bump was actually for gay rights." See Photo and read the article at TheDailyDot.com/politics/Obama fist bumping/ Franklin barbeque. Instead of flying down to Laredo or any other crossing site on the Mexican Border, Obama was gathering attention for one of his favorite causes, the promotion of sodomy, same sex relationships, and those who engage in those acts.

This is the same Pharaoh Obama I who rushes to make calls to any athlete who announces his preference for sex with other males. Anytime there is an opportunity to promote, celebrate or to endorse homosexuality our beloved President will do that. At the Democratic Convention, cameras were aimed at the rear of the podium while the speaker announced, to an uproarious applause, the "progress" made during the Obama years for gay rights and same sex marriage. As that announcement was made the President was actually doing a little dance step behind the speaker.

I have wondered what The President of the United States says to a recently "outed" homosexual. I imagine the conversation goes something like this, "Congratulations on having the courage and integrity to announce that you are gay. I myself will make a similar announcement soon after my terms in office end." Obama's homosexuality is documented and sometimes those testimonies must be anonymous.

They are anonymous because all members of Jeremiah Wright's Trinity Church know that two men were executed, Chicago-Gangland-style, for their homosexual involvement with Candidate Obama, and that will be described in the next paragraph.

My primary source for collecting information on the homosexual activities of Pharaoh Obama before he even ran for Congress comes from a series of articles written by Jerome Corsi for WND. Author Corsi speculates that Obama joined Jeremiah Wright's Church with no intention of increasing his relationship with Jesus Christ. Obama was seeking a political refuge and a springboard. He knew that as an active homosexual he could find what was called a "beard" or cover for his homosexuality in Pastor Wright's so called "down low club." The purpose of that group had nothing to do with leading black men out of their sin of homosexuality but provided cover stories for black men wanting to remain homosexuals while concealing their homosexual activity. Some have called the Wright group a match service because the group found women for homosexual men to marry, thereby providing a cover story for their homosexuality.

After entering into the heavy homosexual milieu at Trinity Church Candidate Obama developed relationships with 25 year old Larry Brand and a more visible relationship with Choir Director, 47 year old Donald Young. Larry Brand was the first homosexual partner of Obama's to die, and he was found dead in his apartment murdered by multiple gunshots. Then, only a few weeks later, on December 24, 2008, Donald Young was executed by multiple gunshots in his Chicago apartment. Nothing was taken from his dwelling, and his murder was clearly a gang-style execution.

The violent murders had the effect of silencing members of the congregation who knew what had been going on, and probably knew forensic details about the murders.   Jerome Corsi has interviewed many members of Trinity Church and all correspondents have insisted, for obvious reasons. that their testimonies be anonymous.

The Down Low members of Trinity Church arranged Obama's marriage to Michelle Robinson, who had been partially raised in the household of Jessie Jackson. The difference between the philandering of JFK and of Bill Clinton, and of Barack Obama is that the Obama attempt at deception was designed and manufactured institutionally (Through the Down Low Club,) while JFK and Clinton managed to get by through silence and adlibbing lies. While the real story behind Pharaoh Obama's identity and his sexual preferences are held as tightly closeted information, by the powers that be and a huge majority of the press, the fact remains that who he is and what he does, are great, dark secrets.

In fact the lies used to construct the Obama mystique are so blatantly outrageous that it seems incredulous that his misbehavior has remained secret from so many for so long. That is because the Obama administration, some way or another has managed to control the liberal media to a ridiculous degree. In the old vernacular from the 1920s and the 1930s in the Chicago criminal culture it was said that criminals such as Al Capone, "owned" certain institutions such as the courts, the press or law enforcement. Recall that the famous crime busters in that culture of criminality were called, "The Untouchables," officers of the law immune to attempts to secretly work for the criminals, men of integrity who could not be bought.

I also believe that modern liberals have eyes but cannot see, and have ears and cannot hear because of the perception disorder described by Paul as a condition imposed by God in II Thessalonians 2:11-12, "And for this cause God shall send them strong delusion, that they should believe a lie. That they might all be damned who believed not the truth but had pleasure in unrighteousness."

WHY BENGHAZI WAS MAYBE AS MUCH AS 100 TIMES MORE SERIOUS A CASE OF DERILICTION OF DUTY THAN WATERGATE

Do you remember Watergate? Talk about a media circus. The pressure generated by the media over Watergate, caused President Nixon to do all that he thought he could possibly do, to get on a helicopter and fly off into the sunset. Understand what actually happened, what the scurrilous crime perpetrated by the Watergate Gang actually was. A small group of men, broke into an office and stole documents related to Democratic Political Strategy. Compare that crime to the dereliction of duty displayed by our Commander-In-Chief during the Benghazi Affair, and Watergate shrinks down to a the status of a College Fraternity Prank, executed with the same sort of daring that young men would use to drive them to participate in a panty-raid. At the Watergate crime scene, things which did not belong to the burglars were taken. At Benghazi lives were lost because Pharaoh Obama flew off to play golf and raise political funds, while servants of the United States of America were pleading for rescue that could have and most certainly should have saved their very lives.

Citizens in harm's way enjoy a sense of security knowing that the men and women who placed them in danger would not ever, by the rules of tradition and common decency ignore their call for help and simply walk away from their duty of protecting the human assets of our Nation. Readers it is evident from all I know about Barack Obama that he has very little respect for American tradition, and perhaps even less common decency. When the chips were down, way down, and an embassy in Libya was being overrun, President Obama ignored an urgent SOS sent out by the Ambassador of that Embassy, and ignored the calls for help with the arrogance one would only expect from a sworn enemy of our Nation.

I can lean on my own combat experiences to try and explain the profound betrayal of Pharaoh Obama I when Ambassador Stevens looked out his window, saw a terrorist mob overrunning the gates of the Embassy he was assigned to command, and made his call for help, for immediate extraction of himself and the remaining members of his staff. To arrogantly turn away from the calls for rescue from the beleaguered Embassy, and to casually jet off to play golf, abandoning the emergency communications and the situation in progress at the White House is like taking a complaining child, locking him in a swelteringly hot car and going off to work. The truth is that moderately decent people don't do things like that, not ever. In a fair and equitable world President Obama would be charged with murder for ignoring the distress calls from the Embassy in Benghazi. In a fair world he would be tried, found guilty of multiple counts of murder, and left to a fate such as the staff around Ambassador Stevens experienced during their final moments of life.

In 1965 I led a Recon Platoon in the Second of the Fifth Battalion of the First Cavalry Division. I often led my 33 man platoon out to distances of 20 miles from the main body of our Battalion. We would either walk out and away from the Battalion or be air-lifted to a distant location via helicopters. Sometimes we would spend several days patrolling an area, searching for signs of enemy activity. On our daily patrols I was confident in two remarkable assets available to me. I could call in air-strikes, artillery barrages, or helicopter gunships by picking up the handset of my PRC-25 radio and saying, "Chickasaw 6, this is Cool Bandit 6." Most of the time a Master Sergeant back at the tent, housing the leadership of the Battalion would respond within seconds, with "Cool Bandit six this is Chickasaw 6-5." If something out of the ordinary or of an urgent nature was in progress then our Battalion Commander, Lieutenant Colonel Robert Tully would answer the call with, "Cool Bandit 6 this is Chickasaw 6, over." In those days I often thought of the fire support at my command as the wrath of God. I could make a call and within seconds the thump, thump, thumping sound of heavy ordinance artillery shells pounding into the earth could be heard close to us.

The other thing that filled my young heart with confidence and a safe and secure feeling of security, like a baby tucked into a warm bed by loving parents, was the knowledge that we could leave the scene, and be lifted up and out of any situation we didn't want to be in on that particular day. We always had an extraction plan, a bug-out plan. I was always looking for a place where five Huey Helicopters could land and take us back to the Battalion area for hot food and coffee. As long as I had a working radio and a landing zone which could be our extraction point, I was large and in charge, walking through the valley of death with a surety that the enemy, regardless of his size, was no match for our Recon Platoon. My sentiment for the enemy in those days was so well expressed in a standard expression of the fictional TV Character, Mr. T, who often said, "I pity the fool." I thought like most Junior Officers of the First Cav. We had bought the T-shirts and drank the Kool-Aid regarding the capabilities we had.

A few years later, during my second tour in Viet Nam, I worked for the CIA's Phoenix Project. Those CIA men liked to joke and say, "I don't have to put up with this s---. I got my cyanide pill and I can quit any time I want.' As long as we could make it to our extraction point we had complete mobility, a way out of the toughest situation, a bug-out plan.

Our mobility was all based on the fact that our Leaders and Commanders were always, any time of the bright sunny days or the long dark nights, standing by, at their posts, ready to do whatever was needed to bring us though our assigned mission and back to the base camp. Colonel Tully always pops quickly into my mind when I think of leadership. He was the great man of courage and absolute integrity I knew and so passionately admired, because he did his job, every day and in every way. I cannot even imagine Colonel Tully simply turning his back and walking away like a worthless coward. The betrayal of the Embassy staff in Benghazi must have come crashing down on those men like a giant sledge hammer from heaven.

Most assuredly the embassy staff had an extraction plan. That plan was one of the first things any staff member would have wanted to know when he or she reported for duty in Benghazi. Every member would have known that if an extraction were necessary he or she would move quickly to the extraction point, probably on a roof or a garden in the compound. The helicopters would have appeared, landing, perhaps one at a time on a basketball court, and the staff would have been lifted up and away from the chaos beneath them. That is the way things work, and even to imagine that the man at the very top, President Obama would be doing his own version of a bug-out plan, not running from physical danger, but escaping from a responsibility he had no intention of accepting, should be unthinkable.

I am astonished at the level of arrogance displayed by Pharaoh Obama I, in simply turning his back on his sacred duty to protect his own! This is the same level of arrogance Mr. Obama used for years to ignore all requests to show us his birth certificate. He had no pleasant answer to the accusations regarding his total ineligibility to Command, so he simply ignored the requests, demands and court orders.

Not only is the arrogance of President Obama a spectacular thing, but there is an amazing wonder in the blind and ridiculous acceptance of whatever the Pharaoh announces, by the Liberals who love him. I believe that blind obedience to nonsense is part of God's curse of America, described succinctly in II Thessalonians 2: 11-12, *"For this cause God shall send them strong delusion, that they should believe a lie: That they all might be damned who believed not the truth, but had pleasure in unrighteousness."*

In the earliest days of the Benghazi debacle there was a lie floating around that the overrunning of the Embassy had nothing to do with a Terrorist Plot to take down the Embassy, but was a reaction to a cheap and horrible-quality film an American had made depicting Mohammed as a Pedophile and the Islamic Religion as bad fairy tales. Many claim that Hillary Clinton was in on the rejection of any idea of taking responsible action in response to the calls from the Embassy for help. Others say she was opposed. I don't know what to think because there are so many versions of the story. Liberals use a technique they teach in Military Intelligence Classes. It is a sophisticated protocol for lying called misinformation.

The media publishes all kinds of stories and those stories are not even intended to inform or to educate, but to confuse. Because the liberal media is in on the lying and the grandiose attempts to deceive on issues such as Barack Obama's phony birth story and his manufactured educational credentials, the IRS Scandal, and the Benghazi cover-up (Which included firing a crowd of Military General Officers who would not support the Democratic Lies of what really happened at Benghazi) it is most difficult to dig through all of the misinformation and blatant lies and come up with true accounts of what has been happening.

One of those military officers who was purged by the Obama administration was retired Navy Captain Joseph John who said, "I believe there are more than 137 officers who have been forced out or given bad evaluation reports so they will never make Flag (officer,) because of their failure to comply to certain views. Retired Army Major General Patrick Brady said, "There is no doubt that he (President Obama) is intent on emasculating the military and will fire anyone who disagrees with him. Retired Army Lt. General William G. Jerry Boykn said, "Over the past three years, it is unprecedented for the number of four-star generals to be relieved of duty, and not necessarily relieved for cause. A Pentagon Official who asked to remain nameless because they were not authorized to speak on the matter said, "even young officers, down through the ranks have been told not to talk about Obama or the politics of the White House. They are purging everyone, and if you want to keep your job you just keep your mouth shut. Now this trend appears to be accelerating." General Paul Valley said, "Absolutely every communist regime on the planet did this as soon as they got into power. I am surprised that this Communist Traitor with his feet up on our furniture in the White House hasn't done this until now." Please, reader, as you read of 137 high ranking officers and non-commissioned officers, after serving for decades, going wherever they were needed and obediently putting themselves in harm's way, being purged as if they had not served with distinction. Remember also when Joseph Stalin began his reign of terror how he had his enemies, political and military, board a small ship. They were forced to go below decks, the hatches were nailed shut and the boat was sunk.

I believe that Ambassador Stevens was tortured and raped, then after his body was paraded through the streets of Benghazi, his dead body was raped again, by men who are held, by American Liberals as the darling revolutionaries of the Middle East, the Islamic Terrorists. In most Liberal Publications to include TV Reporting, you will seldom see the words "Islamic" and "Terrorist" used together. This protecting of the thugs of Islam is part of the Liberal Lie of how they view the world. Certainly they should be expected to take the Islamic side whenever the winds of conflict blow, because their alleged "Christian" Pharaoh is in fact (according his own "slipped" admission during an interview with George Stephanopoulos) a Muslim, and not a Christian at all. He did say, "My Muslim faith," during an interview on ABC with George Stephanoplolis, back in Sept 2008. You can then hear the interviewer reminding him that he is posing as a Christian and he quickly corrects himself, saying, "My Christian faith." As he mumbles the words, "My Christian Faith," notice that his eyes are down and his voice subdued as if he was in pain calling himself a "Christian."

This is an appropriate place to mention the nature of the mob overrunning the embassy and raping, murdering and then raping the dead body of

Ambassador Stevens on September 11. This was not an orderly operation but a mob uprising of Islamic thugs who murdered Ambassador Stevens and three other staff members.

An article posted on Breithart.com, written on June 4th, 2014 by Debra Heine, was titled: Report: Ambassador Stevens Killed by Lethal Injection After Prisoner Swap Went Bad. In the article it was reported that Bill Gertz, a writer at the Washington Times reported a recent post from an Al Queda Terrorist reporting that Ambassador Stevens was killed by Lethal Injection. That action took place after the invading terrorists at the Benghazi Embassy realized that a planned kidnapping of the Ambassador to be exchanged for high level Islamic Terrorist, who were imprisoned, was not going to work. The invaders then initiated Plan B and killed the Ambassador by lethal injection. This report just might all be malarkey to construct a platform to launch the lie that Ambassador Stevens was murdered by lethal injection. Considering the riotous nature of the terroristic mob I believe the calm and calculated procedure of administering a lethal injection probably is 100% fiction.

Another explanation, even more compatible with the image of good old boys from Benghazi, who were not terrorists at all, is that an autopsy proved that Ambassador Stevens died from smoke inhalation. That wonderfully convenient lie was presented by a panelist, Eleanor Clift, on The McLaughlin Group on May 14, 2014. On that program Panelist Eleanor Clift insisted that Ambassador Stevens was not murdered but died from smoke inhalation. Panelist-for-life Pat Buchanan reminded Ms Clift, "Eleanor it was a terrorist attack." Eleanor Clift continued to speak, not allowing truth to slow down her presentation of what was about to become the Democratic party line; that Ambassador Stevens died from smoke inhalation. That was a good explanation, because it let both the terrorists and Obama off the hook, so the Washington people ran with it. Panelist Clift then repeated her accusation and said that the embassy invasion was all about the stupid video previously mentioned. Ms. Clift revealed her true agenda when she remarked, "If you're going to put somebody on trial, put David Petraeus on trial, not Hilary Clinton." . When Liberals lie, using outrageous stories, those stories are almost always designed to support some liberal Political agenda. Eleanor Clift was talking the nonsense of death by smoke inhalation, merely to keep the public persona of Democratic Candidate Hillary Clinton untarnished, and help Mrs. Clinton to maintain her viability as a presidential candidate.

As so often happens when controversy involving Pharaoh Obama I and his staff arise, documents, such as the autopsy reports, (and birth certificates, college records, and emails from the IRS Offices of former IRS employee, Lois Lerner, etc. etc.) suddenly become "classified," and "unavailable." Eleanor Clift was obviously briefed and prepped to deliver her outrageous accusation that Ambassador Stevens had not been brutally murdered by a terrorist mob, but that he died from smoke inhalation.

Regarding the confusing and conflicting information regarding what happened in Benghazi, Iowa Republican Rep Steve King said "I don't think the public has any idea, and I tell you, I don't either, of the chronology of the events — what took place, and who was where doing what and why. And all the way down through — we still haven't seen an autopsy report on the Ambassador yet. Simple questions that you would ask in the first 24 hours have not been asked yet."

Mr. King reiterated his support for a proposal put forth by Republican Rep. Frank Wolf of Virginia, who has called for a Watergate-style select committee to investigate the circumstances surrounding the attack, in which U.S. Ambassador J. Christopher Stevens, former Navy Seals Glen Doherty and Tyrone Woods, and State Department officer Sean Smith were killed.

LIBERALS HAVE NO SHAME

Shame is a very powerful feeling with the power to restrain man and his behavior. Pop Psychology and modern "self-help" emphasizes the negative aspect of shame because of the limitations it inevitably puts on man and what he can or cannot achieve. Here then is something you probably have not read or heard; a few words on why shame is essential to life. Freedom without the tempering aspects of shame is chaos, people responding without any restraining willpower to their every whim. Adam and Eve ran when they realized that they were naked, and the shame of their nakedness drove them to run, and to quickly improvise methods for covering themselves.

In the best of times and circumstances, Man is able to restrain himself, and to keep a hands-off posture regarding his neighbor's wife and his neighbor's property. Without a real respect for the shame that comes from violating the boundaries of others, many men would simply respond to their most base drives, and publicly assault their neighbor's wife, and take whatever of their neighbor's property they could take without getting caught and suffering prosecution. Man's sense of shame tempers his behavior, and helps him to hold his wildest urges in check.

Watch two boys at play. If Johnny wants Stevie's toy he just might strike him in the face, and snatch that toy away for himself. If the ancient and dying art of parenting is available, a parent will insist that Johnny returns the toy to Stevie and apologize to him. There might even be a statement such as, "You ought to be ashamed." Sorry to all my humanist friends, but this old Counselor believes the admonition is true, accurate and appropriate. Johnny should indeed be ashamed because hitting people and taking their stuff, and doing those things, is far more destructive than feeling ashamed of doing those things.

One of the things that makes Liberals such destructive adversaries is that many of them stumble through life, shame-free, with no regret for savaging the character or property of their enemies. Most of this chapter has been dedicated to making the case that Liberals lie. They lie often and they do so without any apparent sense of shame. They recognize no restraining factor in their lying. They lie because they can get away with it and because they believe it serves their immediate purpose. They are shameless in their deceit.

If I am correct the people leading the liberals of America are doing their dirty work without any apparent sense of honor or shame. That means that a Liberal response to any given situation will have nothing to do with the guidance of the Constitution they swore to defend, common decency, or for the good and the future of our Nation. No siree, they are shame-free rascals and everything they say or do is driven by the same selfish question, "What's in it for me?"

We Americans cherish our right to do spiritual and intellectual battle over issues, because most of us believe it will all come down to in the next election, will be what "The People" decide and express through their votes. Before you take a deep relaxing breath and rest easy because you know we can change things at the polls, remember that the Liberals have no shame, and are very busy wrecking and "fixing" the election process.

The most obvious tactic in fixing America's elections is the flooding of our southern states with illegal aliens. That project is essentially a ruse to flood America with about 20 million new Democratic Voters. There are other reasons for promoting illegal immigration, such as the overloading of our healthcare and government assistance programs, and I will discuss those in a future chapter titled, "Anarchy, Premeditated Treachery."

An Organization named, "Judicial Watch," was instrumental in having 50,000 names of voters removed from the voting rolls in Florida. In a Wall Street Journal Opinion, written by Robert D. Popper, in April 2014 the article reported that a February 2012 Report, released by the Pew Charitable Trusts, revealed that 1.8 million deceased registrants were listed as active voters, and that 2.75 million voters had active registrations in more than one State. The same study reported that the myth that Voter ID Laws suppress voting, does not exist, and has never been studied or documented. Here then are the unifying aspects of the 50,000 voters whose names were removed from the rolls of active voters in Florida:

1.   Each of them was dead, in the ground, with ten toes pointed to the sky.

2.   Each of them was a Democratic Voter.

Unbelievingly, The white House protested the

removal of those names from the rolls in Florida.

LIBERAL LYING 101; HOW THEY CONSTRUCT AND DEVELOP A LIE

Liberals lie, and they lie when the truth would be so much easier. The Problem is that their mischievous behavior is so rampant that they need to lie, and lie often to conceal who they actually are and that they are doing. Here then are observations of lying from JFK to Obama. This is the pattern I have observed.

STEP ONE: Play Stupid; Ignore the problem for as long as you can and if nobody says anything, then forget about it.

STEP TWO: Launch a flood of misinformation. If nobody buys off on the fact that your hands are clean of any and all guilt, release as many conflicting reports as possible, such as phony birth certificates, tales of missing emails, or stories about how our murdered public servants died from lethal injection or smoke inhalation. Make sure that so many versions of the story are released that anyone and everyone is thoroughly confused.

STEP THREE: After stonewalling things for from 6 to 9 months release an official party line story. Brief everyone, the media and your own staff, and hold them to the story you have designed for them. If you can get them chanting about something such as "weapons of mass destruction," then you have won, even though the weapons of mass destruction could have been as small as a briefcase, and were easily concealed from any army of inspectors, or sent out by overnight express to Syria,

STEP FOUR: Attack any opposition forces, claiming they hate you, want to victimize you and are telling their own elaborate lies. If you are not a white male, demand that the attack is a personal and either a racial, or sexual attack against you.

STEP FIVE: Tell your lies over and over for about a year and after two years have passed, declare the whole incident to be "Ancient History," a story so old and worn that only silly folk even mention it. Laugh it up every chance you get. Make jokes about such idiots as the rubes still demanding to see your birth certificate or college transcripts. Instead of actually dealing with the problem laugh it up, ridicule your attackers and have the press come to your aid, proclaiming anyone who resists the lie of your story as an imbecile.

STEP SIX: Keep lying and covering up because after two years you will certainly have three or four more enormous lies you need to develop.

SOME IMPORTANT POINTS FROM
THIS CHAPTER

1. Liberals lie.

2. Liberals will do anything, no matter how immoral it is, to win.

3. Liberals recognize no wrong in their own dishonesty, and magnify any mistake by conservatives as game-changing and behavior worthy of immediate banning, and shunning. An example of this tactic came in the public shaming of Pat Buchanan who was characterized as a Jew-Hating bigot.

4. Liberals cannot perceive that any of their kind could or would ever do anything wrong.

5. Liberals have lost sight of any difference between moral and immoral. Instead of judging a statement by its' degree of truth, they judge all communication by what it does for "me and my cause".

CHAPTER FOUR

The New Godless America

"The whole difference between construction and creation is exactly this: that a thing constructed can only be loved after it is constructed; but a thing created is loved before it exists." **-Charles Dickens**

"Little Children, it is the last time: and ye have heard that antichrist shall come, even now are there many antichrists; whereby ye kniow that it is the last time," **I John 2:18**

WHY WE SPENT BILLIONS ON A

"SUPER COLLIDER"

The clichéd joke has been told many times of the atheist who confronted God claiming that he could create a universe.

God said, "Go ahead and try."

When the atheist bent over to pick up a scoop of dirt, God interrupted him, saying, "No, no. Use your own dirt."

That silly story illustrates the dilemma of all those who want to eliminate God from "the beginning," suggesting that there is no actual "intelligent design" involved in the creation (They would much prefer to call it origins) of the Universe. Instead they persist in the so-called, "Big-Bang" theory, which is one of the most implausible and ridiculous explanations for the existence of the universe ever concocted.

Former Pastor of the First Baptist Church of Dallas, Mac Brunson, said something like this about the theory of evolution. He said that if you were to take a single screw and cause it to pass very, very slowly through an aircraft factory over a few hundred million years that the odds of it exiting that factory after having "evolved" into a fully functional 747 aircraft, with over a million working parts, were better than the odds of the human body having evolved from a single cell animal, considering the human body is a complex assembly of trillions of parts called cells, that with each breath displays trillions of highly complex interactions in order to sustain life.

Man, meanwhile, continues to promote his "big-bang" theory of nonsense. The advantage of the big bang silliness is that it allows man to claim that there is no God, and that there was no "intelligent design" involved in the creation of the universe. God-haters must go to ridiculous extremes to "prove" that God does not exist, because the proof of God's existence is in every cell in every living thing on earth. As Og Mandino said, "If one doubts the existence of God he needs only to look at a tree."

Now I want to write a few words about the efforts of many Americans to prove that God wasn't even needed during the creation of the universe. In 1987 Congress was told by a large and impressive group of renowned scientists and engineers that, for a mere Four Billion dollars, those men could reconstruct the Big-Bang. The machine they began to construct came to be called the Super-Collider.

Congress was later told that to do things right the super collider would cost over ten billion dollars. By October 21st, 1993 two billion had already been spent and the result was a tunnel near Waxahachie, Texas approximately 21 miles long. I was driving that day, listening to a talk show on my car radio. I remember an interview the host of that program had with one of the top scientists from Super Collider Project. Both men were lamenting that the Congress had terminated the funding of the Super Collider. The scientist explained what the closing of that program was going to cost the scientific community. He said something like this, "We know what happened during the Big Bang, and we know a lot about what happened during the time after the first 44 one hundredths of a second. The Super-Collider was designed to show us what happened during the first 44 one hundredths of a second." The man on the radio was describing the Big-Bang as a fact, something that had certainly happened, "in the beginning."

The scientist was describing what the Super-Collider had been designed to achieve. Scientists on that project were hoping that by smashing protons together, traveling at close to the speed of light, they would recreate the Big-Bang and lead them to discover the theoretical element known as the "God Particle, " described in a Book by Leon Lederman titled, THE GOD PARTICLE: If the Universe is the answer, what is the question? Some scientists believe that an elusive (and still theoretical) particle contains "the element responsible for making the Universe back when that bucket of dirt exploded. This particle is known as The Higgs Boson Particle. Don't expect anyone to show you a thimble full of Higgs-Boson Particle, because it probably doesn't exist, and if it does it is absolutely not responsible for the design and construction of our universe.

We Christians are so very fortunate, because by our Faith, we don't merely believe, we know, how the world was created. It's all clearly explained in the first five words of the Bible, Genesis 1:1, "In the beginning, God created..." That's it? Yes, that's it! That's all I need because I also believe in this thing known as Biblical inerrancy. If it's in the Bible it is a fact as far as I am concerned. See what I just did? I saved the expense of spending Billions of Dollars to prove that the power to create is with God alone, and I don't need to discover the power of a Higgs-Boson Particle nobody has been able to put in a jar yet... See readers, all of the scientific research (Real science, not this chase after an elusive but still not found "god-particle") has had its say, we still have tons of real evidence that man and all that is was created by God.

While I am at it let me just state that, as a writer, I really don't like it when people casually throw the word "create" around with no understanding of, or respect for what it is. Create means to make from nothing, and man in all of history, has never created anything the size of a Higgs-Boson Particle, nothing. To say that man "creates" anything is giving him credit for what he has never and will never achieve. God meanwhile reached out into nowhere, took a heap of nothing and created, from that, everything. That is what happened, and that is all I need to prove it happened, just as it is explained in the first chapter of Genesis.

So here are the only two theories available on how we got here (we being, me, you and all humans, along with all plants, animals and all this planet and other bodies of real property somewhere or anywhere in space, all matter and all chemicals to include the air we breathe. I hope I didn't leave anybody or anything out of that brief list) and you might notice that I did not include the god particle-the never seen, touched, nor captured Higgs-Boson Particle. I left that one out because it probably doesn't exist and is only some late night imagining of some God-Hating scientists.

We were either created, as we can all read in the first five words of Genesis...or...some shovel full of dirt somehow mysteriously came together and because of the creative power of the god-particle in that dirt, the dirt exploded and became the Universe, with all of the infinite complexity of nature, with all of the plans in place for the evolving of mankind that includes some very tiny and very complex DNA that our daddies (Who were sperm donating men) gave to our mommies (Who were sperm receiving and baby making human machines) and Voila! Here we are in this wonderland called Earth, serving an awesome God and headed for eternity with Him in this real place called Heaven, which is so spectacular that not a one of us can come close to even imagining what it is like. The exceptions to that last statement are people who hate our awesome God, stubbornly stumble through life without Him, often committing suicide because of the utter futility of life, and are headed for an eternity of torment in a place called Hell. Those are your two choices, and if you have a few functioning brain cells you can discern that we were all created, and that Big-Bang malarkey is an excuse to claim that there is no God for the God-haters, many of whom in America, are known as Democrats or Liberals.

So guess which one of those two theories the so called main-stream people choose? Ready? They celebrate the birthday of Darwin, the weird and peculiar man who came up with the whole evolution excuse for godliness. That's right. S.E. Cupp writes in her Book, "LOSING OUR RELIGION; The Liberal Media's Attack on Christianity:, "For Liberals Darwin is the antidote for Jesus, quite literally the ANTI-Christ, and those who criticize his theory of evolution are part of a still evolving fringe minority of Bible-thumpers and rednecks." I share Ann Coulter's belief as she wrote in her Book, Godless; The Church of Liberalism, ""The Liberal's myth is Charles Darwin's theory of evolution, which is about one notch above Scientology in scientific rigor. Not only is creationism (Notice I did not call creationism a theory) discarded, it is ridiculed as if it were some low form of contaminated matter, capable of making people sick or stupid. Joy Behar from "THE VIEW, actually said that a parent who teaches children about creationism is practicing "Child abuse." The thing you need to remember about the theory of evolution is that it has nothing to do with a scientific explanation of how the world began, but that it is a political yarn used to disprove the existence of "Intelligent Design," or of the one and only God, who could have orchestrated that intelligent design.

That Big-Bang story is so sloppily constructed that it makes liberal liars look really amateurish and not very intelligent at all. They probably latched onto the Big-Bang nonsense because of a theory they have held for centuries about how order proceeds out of chaos. A German Philosopher, Georg Wilhelm Fredric Hegel is accredited with launching a belief that order evolves naturally out of chaos. In the next chapter I will explain how Liberal anarchists use the Hegelian Dialect to plan the chaos they cherish so dearly. They love the chaotic state so much that their plans dictate that if there is no naturally occurring chaos, they themselves will generate it.

Hegel was influential on Marx, the co-author, along with Frederich Engels, (actually Marx wrote almost all of the founding documents of Communism) of the Communist Manifesto. Karl Marx was not just an atheist, he was a full-blown Satanist. During his college days he wrote mushy poems about the true love of his life, whom he identified as Lucifer. Not surprisingly the Communist Manifesto calls for the abolishing of religion and of the ownership of property. Once the people are made financially impotent, then they only need to have God removed from their lives so the state (in our case that would be Pharaoh I and his Czars and confidants) can move in and control every aspect of society. I have previously stated that Obama boasted about his work in seeking out the godless and very ruthless Marxist Professors. What a waste of human energy that was!

I use the term ruthless, based on historical evidence that Stalin murdered about 70 Million, while Chairman Mao killed about 200 million and Pol Pot had a small country for a short time and only managed to fill his infamous killing fields with about a million bodies. **6.**

LIBERALISM; CHURCHILL NAILED IT

Churchill nailed it, dead center, when he described a Liberal as "a man with both feet planted firmly in the air." As far as intention goes, the liberals have the very best of those, great ideas worthy of the best of noble men, only their application of those good intentions resembles the proverbial monkey in the tree with a machine gun.

Here is one case illustrating what I just wrote. After Hurricane Katrina there were urgent needs all over Southern Louisiana. The collective hearts of the Liberal Democrats in Washington were collectively broken, so they sent money, millions of dollars to Louisiana. The problem is that they sent that money through channels and not directly to the thousands who really needed help. Because the money had to pass through the greed-driven fists of a few dozen Democrats, it never reached the people who genuinely needed that help. There were great intentions with an incredibly ill-conceived delivery system. There is another story about 'helping' Katrina "victims" and it sounded so wonderfully fair and helpful, when we first heard about it. President George Bush went on National Television and announced that he wanted to simply distribute checks for a thousand dollars to those who needed help. That signaled one of the most enthusiastic runs on strip joints in Louisiana and Texas ever witnessed. That beautifully intentioned rescue money wound up being stuffed into the g-string thongs of a few hundred fabric-free dancers.

That essentially identifies the problem; good intentions without an intelligent and workable delivery program aren't worth the fortune cookies where they first appeared. LBJ correctly launched his war on poverty, but he did it with all the aplomb of a 400 pound fat man attempting to dance the lead in Swan Lake in a tutu. Instead of giving away housing, that would be irreparably trashed in a decade, he could have opened tutoring centers and helped minorities get into and through education programs. Meanwhile his marvelous intentions resulted in the construction of a great mass of humanity who, with the help of organizations such as Acorn, have made careers out of ripping off government programs for all there is to be had, through those programs.

Right now, stop and think about the racism that drives the Democratic give-away programs. All the help given to minorities had to begin with a self-centered and racist assumption of, "Those people can't make it by themselves, so we white Liberals will just have to do it for them." The liberal giveaways almost always begin with a belief that those being helped are not capable of helping themselves.

In the following paragraphs I will touch on how the very best and most praiseworthy intentions of Liberal Politicians have resulted in nothing but heartaches and stupendous waste. I will briefly touch on the chaos that has been constructed in our Education System, and has evolved in our families, courts, and in our armed forces. We all began with the intention of finding peace and love and spreading it wherever it was most needed, but we wound up with a nation of integrity-free cutthroats and cheats, who rob and plunder with pens and copying machines instead of short swords and rapiers. I have already written in this Chapter about how the Liberals in America have contributed tremendous energy to their effort to remove God from the great equation we call life, with a flimsy yarn they call "The Big-Bang Theory." Now let's briefly consider how all of that nonsense fails to work.

GOD HATING DEMOCRATS GO PUBLIC AT THEIR CONVENTION

The proverbial cat got out of the bag at the Democratic Convention as Democrats gave America a glimpse into how God-Hating permeates their ranks. A vote was held, officiated by Convention Chairman and the Mayor of Los Angeles, Antonio Villaraigosa, to determine if the Democrats would even allow the G-Word (God) to be used in their official platform documents. The Chairman called for a voice vote, and the first two times he did that, he could not tell which group had carried the vote, the 'yeahs' or the 'nays'. After the third voice vote, he awarded victory to the 'yeahs' and the Democrats thereby officially determined that it would be acceptable to use the G-Word in their documents.

Whether or not the Democrats actually had a majority voting to use the G-Word has been debated passionately. During the voting, C Span Cameras focused on one couple who were highly animated in their opposition to the use of the word God. When the Chairman announced that the measure had passed, the bearded man on camera jumped out of his seat, shaking his fist at the podium, obviously upset and strongly opposed to even the mention of God on any Democratic Documents. That man, along with what sounded like more than half of the delegates, booed loudly, protesting the use of the word, "God." If I worked in central casting and needed to hire a man to portray an obnoxious little, hairy faced anarchist I would find that guy who was shaking his fist at the Podium. Yup, he looked like what most of us think of when we hear the word anarchist. Here, reader, is our great challenge. Because of the instructions Jesus Christ left us with, we must, absolutely must, forgive that guy, and pray for him (and the female person who sat beside him). I think of that chore like this; I surely wouldn't want to spend eternity in Hell with him as a next door neighbor. So I have to forgive him, pray that God gives me a mighty rush of Spiritual Strength and Stamina so I can actually love that man.

The next day, after the Democrats booed God, I received a phone call from a life-long friend. My friend retired from Teaching where he had served as a football coach, teacher, principal and finally as a Superintendent of Schools. I ask that you join me in thinking of that friend of mine as a typical American, Mr. John Q. Public. He was calling about what he had witnessed on TV from the Democratic Convention. He said, with emotions of disgust and lingering disbelief, apparent in his voice, "Marvin, they booed God. They actually booed God!"

Yes, America, we all need to understand that the Democrats revealed the darkness of their God-despising hearts. They are the mob who booed God. May God have mercy on us all, for what so many Americans have become.

AMERICA'S SCHOOLS; READING, WRITING AND MASTURBATION

I'll begin this section with ancient history, going back to 1994 when Bill Clinton's then Surgeon General, Joycelyn Elders, was invited to speak to the wee ones in a kindergarten class. Surgeon General Elders arrived looking elegant and official in a military uniform, complete with campaign ribbons. She then proceeded to tell those small children about masturbation! The only thing I have seen in the defense of the

Surgeon General, is that she was telling people that masturbation was a good thing because she saw it as a deterrent to the spread of Aids.

The far superior deterrent to Aids is sexual abstinence, and that just doesn't play into any Liberal agenda, because it could be construed to be behavior regulated by Biblical Morality. Bill Bennett spoke once on the effectiveness of abstinence in preventing both unwanted pregnancies and the spread of disease, saying, "It (Abstinence) works every time it is used.." President Clinton was unable to protect his Surgeon General from the storm of protests following the news of what she had been telling the tiniest victims of public school education. Reluctantly, President Clinton fired Joycelyn Elders, along with a personal apology to her.

You will not appreciate what Joycelyn Elders did in that small classroom, talking to those small children until you personalize the event. Imagine that you have supervised teeth brushing, breakfast eating, hopefully morning prayers, and the dressing of your very own and very dear six year old sweetie pie and sent him or her off to school. Then you find that this woman dressed like a Naval Admiral, came into the room where your child was supposed to be learning to count to ten and sing the Alphabet song, and she told them about the joys of masturbating. Isn't that your job, to be handled with all of your religious and spiritual beliefs employed by you, and your spouse? Yes it is, and your job has been stolen from you by the aforementioned woman/Admiral, and that isn't why you sent your dear and beloved child to school at all!

Liberals take great advantage of the children in their classrooms, and most of them who are called teachers, conceptualize those classrooms as places for them to have their way with the hearts and minds of your children, packing their heads with the dark, Liberal nonsense of such things as safe sex, god-hating, and the learning of a very twisted understanding of their country and how it was stolen by wicked men such as Washington, Jefferson and Adams, all wealthy exploiters of the poor, ruthless opportunists, who despised the poor and most assuredly the Indians.

Don't blame all of the mischief going on in America's Public Schools on the existing crop of Liberals. They were taught these things by the Liberals who came before them. Marx wrote of the family as an exploitive source of child labor (Slavery) perpetrated by those cruel masters we always thought of as parents. Marx promised his devotees that Communism would destroy the inherent cruelties and abuses in the families of a Nation, and replace them with the orderly education and virtual raising of children by those good old folks in your public school systems.

Keep in mind folks, I am not writing about real teachers such as some of us can recall from a long time ago, in America, men and women who actually taught us math, science, and language skills (to be fair, there are still a handful of real teachers, today, who bravely teach (y)our children the truth, as well as citizenship and manners, in spite of the fact that many texts have been rewritten, using more liberal guidelines and then substituted for former texts). Those old relics from long ago even taught things such as how noble, courageous and valiant, men such as George Washington and a few others were!

The Communists were God-haters and their hatred extended to everything God had created and provided for man and mankind. That hatred included the family, which Marx and Engels wanted to abolish. There are obvious things a family provides, such as a basic education in the cultural behaviors a child must master in order to live in an organized society. The Communists wanted those educational responsibilities taken away from the families, which they viewed only as slavery for children. They were quick to suggest that the functions of the family could easily be replaced with public education and publicly administered prostitution!

When I write "public education" do not be fooled by visualizing an old public school building where you were taught traditional subjects such as reading, writing and math. Hillary Clinton hinted at the education she and Marxist Liberals want for our children in her 2006 Book, *IT TAKES A VILLAGE*, what she did not mention in her book, was that Liberals want far more than a world where many. many people are involved in the raising of children. They want children removed from their parents and from the influences of home!

God only knows what goes on in homes, behind closed doors. Parents might actually be telling their children about the Bible and teaching them Biblical principles! The poor babies might grow into adulthood not knowing that dating protocols included any kind of sexual activity the child might feel like (s)he needed, as long as "safe sex," was practiced. The very inappropriately named "Safe-Sex" sacrament of Liberal 'liberating' education clearly does not work!

My wife and I were substituting in a special needs classroom in Dallas, with some very disturbed young children ranging from 10 years old and upward. One afternoon, a clearly blatant homosexual man came to distribute neon colored condoms to those children aged ten and up, (who were challenged just to find their way to school each day) and were not even qualified to practice "safe sex"!

Liberals get very excited about opportunities to "teach" our children. This old man's advice is to home school your children whenever possible. In the now sacred privacy of your own homes you can still stand with your children before a video screen, as they pledge allegiance to the flag, one Nation <u>under God</u>. They can still begin a day's education with very exciting and relevant stories from the Bible, and they can spend an entire school year without some man or woman coming in to teach them to practice "safe sex".

Proverbs 22:6 teaches us, "Train up a child in the way he should go, and when he is old he will not depart from it." The problem with that wisdom is that with self-loving/adoring Liberals, the "way he should go" is all determined with a seething hatred of God and an acknowledgement that lust is a natural, unavoidable condition of the human spirit. Liberals believe that teaching abstinence to teenagers is a trivial and useless waste of energy. They "know" that teaching teenagers abstinence is futile because they also "know" that "kids are going to do it anyway". Once again I remind you that Liberals believe our children are incapable of moral behavior, because they themselves are run-away trains in terms of their own moral misbehavior. Remember the defining phrase for Liberals, "Lacking in moral restraint."

I reviewed a half dozen reference books on our Public Schools and each contained parts of a laundry list, or ludicrous events perpetrated by overly-zealous liberal teachers and administrators on our children! Small children have been humiliated after responding to write essays on people who have helped them or people they admire for the apparently 'high crime' of writing about characters described in the Bible.

Students and teachers have been taken to court by the American Civil Liberties Union and forced to pay bankrupting fines for praying, for mentioning God, or for singing songs or reciting poems that even mentioned God! Rather than add to the exhaustive list of the quasi-legal things happening in our schools I will just present a very brief outline of how those nonsensical things work.

Anti-God events in public schools usually begin with some parents who decide to be offended because something as alarming as a small group of students meeting at lunch time, for Bible Studies. They report their angst to the ACLU. The ACLU, with a huge financial war chest, brings suit against the perpetrators, the teachers involved and or the School or School District. Because most courts of our land are stacked with Liberal Judges, the ACLU wins and individuals or institutions are often brought into bankruptcy. Teachers and administrators hear about the nonsense and they immediately determine that they will not suffer similar fates, so they become anti-God crusaders in their own classrooms and schools. The anti-God movement is growing, spreading, essentially trashing our public school system. Understand this; When God is formally asked to withdraw from an institution or activity, He will do just that-and that is never a good thing!

A GODLESS AMERICA

Weird Examples of Things Silly, Hideous and Blasphemous

Attempting to purge God, and even the very mention of His Name from events which might offend some ridiculously devout God hater (and yes, God-hating, thanks to the ACLU and our Liberal Courts, has become a religion of its own! If you have doubts, just observe the fervor the God-haters display in their quest to remove God and His name from our culture.) The situation in America today was expressed correctly, when Christian Radio talk-show hostess, Janet Meford, said, "The most respected religious leader in America today is Oprah Winfrey". Ann Coulter defined the problem in the title to one of her books, THE CHURCH OF LIBERALISM; GODLESS.

Honor students were punished when they mentioned God, or, the ultimate offense - actually quoted scripture at graduation ceremonies. Small children have been sent home with warning letters addressed to their parents because they dared to select Biblical heroes for their essays on people they most admired. School districts have been brought to financial ruin through ACLU Law Suites, because they dared to allow public prayer before a football game. This next event is, in this author's opinion, the silliest of the silly, a genuine exercise in trivial pursuit, a shining example of how absurd the God-Haters have become.

My 'silliest of the silly award' has to go to the teacher in the Dyer County High School, in Dyer County, Tennessee. A student in her class said, "Bless you", when one of her classmates sneezed. The teacher responded with saying, we're not going to have God-speaking in this class. After the incident, some of the other students responded by wearing home-made Tee shirts, decorated with the words, "BLESS YOU."

This old man has served as a substitute teacher in several of America's Public Schools, and I have heard some terrible language from students, but among the oral sewage I have heard, "Bless you," was not on my personal list of offensive things said.

DOWNRIGHT HIDEOUS

A man who has the audacity to call himself a pastor, Jeremiah Wright, blasphemed, not only out loud, but actually from behind a pulpit in an alleged Christian Church. Most pastors preach against breaking one of the Ten Commandments (The one that commands that we not take the Lord's Name in vain) and would not dare to break that commandment while standing behind a pulpit, posing as a pastor! You probably have heard this one many times, but in case your TV was stolen several years ago, or you just don't watch it anymore, here is what the man said who pastored the very Church Pharaoh Obama I attended for 20 years: He said, "Not God bless America, no, no, no. God d—n America." That, reader, is the most hideous example of God-hating this old man can imagine.

GODHATERS AS BLASPHEMERS

This example of public blasphemy occurred at the 2010 Soul Tran Awards. Jamie Fox was introduced. He took the microphone, walked out on the stage and said, "I want to thank my Lord and Savior." Then he paused a second or two before identifying who he called "Lord and Savior," as he said, "Barack Obama." Then he marched around the stage chanting, Barak Obama as the crowd applauded loudly. The fact that one man publicly proclaimed that he thought Barack Obama was his Lord and Savior was a wicked thing, but when hundreds applauded then the proof positive became clear, America is lost, and if not, we are all very close to lost!

IMPORTANT POINTS FROM THIS CHAPTER

1. There is a strong God-hating movement in America and it is growing among the Liberals who control our media'

2. Many members of the Democratic Party openly expressed their hatred of God and do not even want His Name mentioned in their official documents.

3. Liberals have attempted to remove "intelligent design" and the part God played in Creation from our text books, by promoting a badly flawed theory of evolution.

4. Liberals seek to destroy the traditional definition of marriage, and include homosexual, same-sex marriage as part of their definition of marriage and of the family.

5. Some Liberals want to use the courts to destroy Christian Family life.

CHAPTER FIVE

PATRIOT OR TRAITOR

(The Chapter With A Guarantee)

(The author guarantees that anyone who reads this chapter will know, without question, the difference between a patriot and a traitor, and be able to identify where he stands and why. Patriot or traitor, Conservative American or Liberal Anarchist? Know the difference and know why you are what you say you are.)

"A nation can survive its fools, and even the ambitious. But it cannot survive treason from within. An enemy at the gates is less formidable, for he is known and carries his banner openly. But the traitor moves amongst those within the gate freely, his sly whispers rustling through all the alleys, heard in the very halls of government itself. For the traitor appears not a traitor; he speaks in accents familiar to his victims, and he wears their face and their arguments, he appeals to the baseness that lies deep in the hearts of all men. He rots the soul of a nation, he works secretly and unknown in the night to undermine the pillars of the city, he infects the body politic so that it can no longer resist. A murderer is less to fear. The traitor is the plague." **Attributed to Cicero Marcus Tullius, spoken in an address to the Roman Senate in 58B.C.**

OLIVER HARDY ON PATROL IN VIET NAM

I've written about this experience I had in Viet Nam already, and it certainly isn't boasting that leads me back to the story. In fact, the event caused me, an Army Ranger, leading a Recon Platoon in the First Cavalry Division, to look a lot more like an Oliver Hardy than a Gary Cooper or a Randolph Scott. We were patrolling in Kon Tum Province, one of the most beautiful spots I have seen on God's green Earth. (I had been told that President Teddy Roosevelt came to Kon Tum to hunt tiger. I had seen a very large tiger track earlier that day, and remember thinking that I did not want to see that cat outside of a zoo cage.) We were walking down a mountain when suddenly I stepped on a very wet and very slick spot of ground, where the sun never made its way through the triple canopy trees and growth above us. My feet were suddenly right in front of my eyes and my rear end was falling to earth. When I hit I immediately began to slide downhill, very fast. For a few seconds it felt a lot like a ride at Six Flags. I went about ten yards and then I went sailing out into the wild blue yonder as I sped across the lip of a cliff. That fall beneath me could have been for hundreds of feet, but God was very good to me that day and the soft red dirt of earth was about four feet beneath my flying body. I looked quickly to my right and there, hunkered down over a small fire, were two North Vietnamese Soldiers, cooking some of the rice they carried in black socks on their backs. Leaning up against the earth on their sides were their Kalashnikov AK-47 rifles.

I often think of the absolute horror those little guys must have felt. I was nothing less than a caricature of a Hulk Hogan leaping from the top rope. Those two men were thinking about nothing but how good that rice was going to taste, when out of nowhere their dining experience was trashed completely by a monster, (a 220 pound American), flying above them, sort of like the Goodyear Blimp over a football stadium. I did what I had been so well trained to do. I turned the M-16 rifle, cradled in my arms, on them, thumbed the selector switch to full automatic and shot.

Those guys were quick, super quick, and by the time I hit the ground they had disappeared. They dropped the flimsy back-packs they had been carrying and evaporated into the thick jungle behind them. I must have hit one of them, because the back-pack he left us had a bullet hole through its' center, and that bullet hole was in the center of every piece of paper in the pack.

We took those back-packs, stuffed with pieces of paper, mostly onion skin paper, with Vietnamese typing. When we got back to our Battalion we turned the back-packs with the papers, over to our Intelligence Officer. He told me he would send it to Division for translating.

About a week later a helicopter brought a Lieutenant from Division Headquarters to our location. He asked if I was Lieutenant Marvin Sprouse. After he identified me he showed me a translation of one of the letters we had captured. The first thing he did was to point out the signature on the paper. It was signed by Ho Chi Minh.

Chairman Ho was a hard-line communist, and like all communists he included a lot of Marxist jargon in his writings. His letter was addressed to all of the valiant revolutionary soldiers of the North (North Vietnamese Army) and of the South (The Viet Cong.)

He congratulated them on their fight against the "puppet government" of the United States. Then he did something unusual. In the style of Willie Joe Namath guaranteeing a Super bowl Victory, Ho Chi Mihn promised his men a victory. He wrote that victory was assured because the most powerful forces in America, the media and Hollywood were on his side! (This letter was written only weeks after Jane Fonda went to Hanoi to harass and to annoy the American POWs and to tell her Uncle Ho how much she admired his communist cause.)

Remember it was 1965 and we had not seen the treachery of Walter Cronkite returning from Viet Nam in 1968, waving the victory flag for the Viet Cong. We had never heard of John Kerry or Bill Clinton, so about all we knew about traitors was that Jane Fonda was a sort of high priestess for the whole anti-American movement. Lady Jane and her friends were doing exactly what Cicero had spoken of over 2,000 years ago; they were rotting the soul of a Nation, our Nation, our beloved America.

By the time I read that letter I had been in Viet Nam for four months, I had already led a detail clearing the bodies of slain Americans from the Battlefield at LZ X-Ray in the Ia Drang Valley. I remember pulling the body of a Lieutenant across that field, and I would see his hand in my dreams for years. He wore a wedding ring and a ring displaying the fact that he had gone through the exhaustive selection process, and endured four very tough years at West Point so that he could wear that tiny gold bar on his collar and lead men into that "valley of death" in Southeast Asia.

Knowing, up close and personal, what some great Americans were giving for their Country in Viet Nam, and then reading that the real enemy was back home in the form of hygienically deprived, pot smoking, draft-dodging, God-hating hippies, who would be waiting when I returned home, to chant about me being a baby killer. It made me angry, sickened me, and revealed the nature of the true enemy of America. Our enemy was not really those courageous and determined Asian guerillas, but the real enemy, the traitors supporting and encouraging Ho Chi Minh and his minions, were back home, drinking hot coffee and lounging around in their air conditioned condos. Thanks a lot, lady-Jane, and I will never forget you and what you have done to this Country I love so dearly.

The greatest insult to me and to all who served, came when the whole country, represented by millions of voters, took one of those war-protesting, traitors and elected him, Bill Clinton, to lead our Nation and to serve as the Commander-in-Chief of our Armed Forces. The late Judge Robert Bork summed the whole thing up so very succinctly when he said, "The Barbarians have gotten tenure."

IF THE NATION HAS NO GREAT PROBLEM INSTALL A PROBLEM FOR THEM

The liberals who would destroy America have definitely got a play book. That play book began way back in 1770 when a man who would become a renowned German Philosopher in the Idealist movement, Georg Hegel was born. Hegel's work would be studied by Marx and Engle and incorporated into the Communist Manifesto. The Heglean Dialect was extracted from Hegel's writings as a method of Government for controlling the masses. It is stated by Heinrich Moritz Chalybäus as comprising three dialectical stages of development:

*A thesis, giving rise to its reaction,

*an antithesis which contradicts or negates the thesis,

*and the tension between the two being resolved by means of a synthesis. 1.

An example of how the principles of the Heleian Dialect might be used in America can be found in the examination of the problem of destroying the 2nd Amendment right of citizens to bear arms. The thesis is the ongoing argument between the citizens who want all guns confiscated and those who want absolutely no restrictions on their right to bear arms.

The Government could stage an antithesis, by equipping and training a shooter and installing that shooter in a firing position with a crowd to use as his targets. (At a mall or sporting event) After he murdered a hundred or more victims, a Government agent could murder him, and the result would be a massive intensification of the arguments regarding the ownership of guns. The Government could then move in with the synthesis, which had been planned from the beginning, and confiscate every privately owned gun in America. A more accessible example of the Hegleian Dialect in action is the monster that could never succeed, The Obamacare Program. The Obamacare Program was deliberately designed to fail and to fail spectacularly.

When Obamacare has caused enough Americans to suffer long enough and hard enough, then the Government will come to the rescue, saving us all from the disaster they tried to install. The solution to a Health Care Program that certainly will fail is the adoption of socialized medicine, with for example, your request to see a doctor for persistent flu symptoms needing to go through the Federal Government.

For those of you who doubt that the Government would dare to be involved in such treachery, consider this infamous quotation from Henry Kissnger. Henry Kissinger in an address to the super-secret Bilderberg Organization meeting at Evian, France, May 21, 1992 said the following as transcribed from a tape recording made by one of the Swiss delegates:

"Today American's would be outraged if U.N. troops entered Los Angeles to restore order; tomorrow they will be grateful. This is especially true if they were told there was an outside threat from beyond, whether real or promulgated, that threatened our very existence. It is then that all peoples of the world will plead with world leaders to deliver them from this evil. The one thing every man fears is the unknown. When presented with this scenario, individual rights will be willingly relinquished for the guarantee of their wellbeing granted to them by their world government." 2.

IS ALL OF THIS JUST TOO "OUT-THERE" TO BELIEVE?

Some will undoubtedly read these words and decide that I am some Bible Thumping, Gun-toting Right Wing nut job and discount all that is written on these pages. Before you join that mob, just consider what has been in progress at our grand centers of learning since the early 80's. Begin with the documented fact that the left, in some venues, prefer socialism over capitalism. Please read this account of what your heroic left-wing crowd did at Columbia University the day President Ragan was shot. This account comes from Wayne Allyn Root who was, at that time a student at Columbia.

"Something extraordinary happened on March 30, 1981 at Columbia University. I was sitting in the biggest political science class at Columbia University, perhaps 200 or more students in a theatre in the round. If Obama was attending Columbia at the time, as he claims, and he was a Political Science major, as he claims, he would almost certainly have been in this class.

On this date in history my hero Ronald Reagan was shot. The reaction in that large political science class that day tells you all you need to know about the media. Because all these years later, when I read Columbia College Today magazine, with updates on my classmates' careers, it is extraordinary how many of them are now leading members of the mainstream media.

As I sat in class that day, listening to the professor lecture, a strange loud noise came from the back of the room. The entire class turned around. The doors in back burst open and a breathless student ran in and screamed, "They just shot Reagan. President Reagan has been assassinated." Can you imagine what the response was at that moment of horror from the future leading members of America's media? Take a wild guess.

A standing ovation. Wild celebration. High fives. Cheering. Fists pounding the air. My classmates were jumping up and down and hugging each other like they had just won the lottery. It was the happiest day of their lives! And I can't forget the words wafting through the air in the midst of this celebration, "YES, they killed that bastard Reagan!" 3.

If the wild-eyed lovers of Marx, Castro, Obama, the death of capitalism in America, and all else that is designed to favor anarchy were only a few nut cases, scattered on a few college campuses, then we could all laugh about them and sleep really well tonight.

The Nut Cases who lust for the total collapse of America and the emergence of their version of sanity in the form of 'one great socialist-big brother, who controls everything' type of government are huge in number, border line insane in their plans for America and squirming with excitement as they watch Pharaoh Obama I do what they know will bring our great Nation crashing down in one great irreparable heap. Most of those God-hating, America-hating mobs are just winging it, constantly complaining about how the government doesn't give them enough to live on to really be counted and to live their own dreams. There is another much more serious and much more dangerous group. Those who would tear our Nation down completely are our very own cadre of anarchists. They went to schools and were taught the finer points of anarchy by a faculty of professors who are so dedicated to the Hegelian concept of Order out of Chaos, they spend their days teaching how to impose Chaos on our Nation and its' people.

PROFESSORS OF CHAOS

In 1996 two Professors in Sociology at Columbia, Richard Andrew Cloward (now diseased,) and his wife, Frances Fox-Piven collaborated on a theory allegedly designed to end poverty in America. The theory behind the plan, now called the Cloward-Piven Strategy, is that if the Government entitlement programs are flooded with impossible demands (too many people to help) then the Government will fail. That failure would result in rioting in the streets, which all communists recognize as a crucial element (They call it revolution) in the establishment of a Communist Government. 4.

There are millions of Americans who prefer what they believe they understand about Socialism or Marxism or Communism, or whatever you want to call a dictatorship based on Marxist principles of enslavement. Most of them have no idea of how former Communist Regimes have failed and how miserable the oppressed and starving people were under those 'Good ole boys of Communism', such as Joseph Stalin, Chairman Mao Tse Dung or Pol Pot. There are some undereducated citizens who believe Castro has made wonderful Utopian improvements in Cuba, but they have not considered that we have not seen a single case of Americans fleeing oppression in Florida and trying to sneak back into Cuba! Castor's military made great sport of shooting holes in boats loaded with Cuban refugees and watching them go down and become shark food. Never mind that many Hollywood brain-dead stars (Is that redundant?) have gone to Cuba to meet their hero, the Great Fidel.

I heard a caller on a radio talk show sum up all of this. He told the host of the program, "America is going down," and he said those words with obvious glee, as if he couldn't wait to watch that happen. At the time I thought that caller sounded a lot like a passenger on the deck of the Titanic rooting for the iceberg. America just might go down and if that happens we will all, every last one of us, hate every minute of it. I promise you that.

The problem I want to shine a bright light on in this book is the criminality of the current crop of politicians in Washington, and how their traitorous behavior has become so pervasive that it can probably not be fixed by installing new politicians and hoping they bring with them to their posts a new integrity and become the 21's Century "untouchables", men and women so dedicated to their professions and so crazy in love with America that they cannot be bought and will simply do the right thing, in the redemption of our once great Nation under God. In the Movie, Braveheart, Mel Gibson, portraying William Wallace said, "There is a difference between us. You think the people of this country exist to provide you with position. I think your position exists to provide those people with freedom." We need, in order to survive the criminal revenging of our Nation under the Obama I Gang, an Army of Bravehearts, a new citizenry, born again in the spirit of our George Washington and those men who saved us from the cutthroats and scoundrels of their day, men hungry for freedom, starving for truth and unshakable in their demand for integrity.

IMPORTANT POINTS FROM THIS CHAPTER

1. America is being trashed not from outside enemies but from within, by well-placed officials who despise America and long to see it in ruin.

2. The teachings regarding order out of Chaos began with Hegel, were carried forward by Marx and are being practiced today by President Obama.

3. The goal of the attempt to destroy America is the installation of Socialism in America.

4. The perpetrators of the plan in progress to destroy America know and appreciate that riots in the streets-a revolution-is necessary to take down America.

5. If America fails, we all will suffer and many will die.

CHAPTER SIX

AMERICA'S THREE GREAT SINS

"Make peace with man and war on your sins,"
Russian Proverb

IDENTIFYING GREAT SIN

About five years ago I attended a conference in Dallas where one of my favorite authors, John McTernan, was scheduled to speak. Dr. McTernan wrote a really important book titled GOD'S FINAL WARNING TO AMERICA. In that Book author McTernan documented dozens of times where great public sin or celebration of sin was met sometimes within hours, and almost always within 24 hours, with violent and destructive acts of God, (hurricanes and tornadoes with the velocity and stamina not seen before in our Country, an earthquake, a wildfire that covered and shut down much of the state of Florida, tornadoes that swept across hundreds of miles, destroying significant parts of cities). In his talk Dr, McTernan used the example of the wildfires that caused highways, including main interstates to be closed in Florida for an entire week. Those fires began almost exactly at 2:00 am, as Disney world was beginning the week-long celebration of Homosexuality, with rainbow Flags decorating their drives and parking lots. A Christian Group gathered and prayed for those people and they prayed until 2:00 a.m. before packing up and leaving. Those fires began almost at exactly the same time the praying stopped. The fires continued for seven days and nights, and then when the Homosexual celebration at Disney World ended, almost to the minute, the rains came and extinguished the fires.

Dr. McTernan documented events which demonstrated the wrath of God, in quick and violent response to sin and celebration, from the mid 80's until he published his Book in 1998.

The day I heard John McTernan speak he said that there were three sins he believed had been the most noticeable in stirring up the wrath of God. He said those three sins were the promotion or celebration of abortion, homosexuality and the mal-treatment of Israel. I am going to write in this Chapter a few paragraphs on each of these three sins, not only because I heard them identified by John McTernan, but because these sins have been elevated to the level of sacramental holiness by the Liberal Religion in America.

ABORTION IS THE MODERN BAAEL WORSHIP

The Israelites had an ongoing on-again-off-again relationship with God (The one God always communicated with a Capital G)and during their times of falling away from God they worshipped a god named Baael, represented by great hollow statues of a god, always with his hands extended, palms up. They built intensely hot fires in the hollow insides of those statues to Baael, and they sacrificed their babies by laying them on the very hot hands of the statues, which had become scorching grills. After giving their babies to be burned alive they participated in drunken sex orgies, with music played loud enough to drown out the pitiful sounds of their babies crying as they died. Some historians speculate that the problem of unwanted pregnancies arose from the drunken sex orgies and the parents, not wanting the inconvenient babies, made up the story of Baael wanting the sacrifice of infants. The so-called sacrifices were actually just a matter of disposing of inconvenient children that just kept coming as the orgies just kept occurring. There never was a god named Baael who demanded the sacrifice of infants, but he did provide a convenient cover story, to justify the murder of infants. 1. (Does this sound familiar to anyone in this Land where we abort about 1.6 million babies each year?) At least the Israelis had a cover story, while today we have to fess-up and admit that we murder for nothing more important than the inconvenience of the birth of a child.

Alan Keyes is, I believe, the most gifted and powerful speaker in America today. Alan Keyes is an outspoken advocate for the unborn, and he bases his very logical argument for their defense on those beautiful words from our own Declaration of Independence. "...we are endowed by the Creator with certain inalienable rights, the right to life, liberty and the pursuit of happiness." Citizens, if we fail to champion and to protect the right to life, then we are a Nation of hypocrites, a squirrelly pack of phonies, all liars.

The most absurd argument for abortion is that it is all about the rights of the women to make a choice regarding her own body. That does not wash at all, simply because the babies being aborted have a population with over half of their number being female, the most defenseless of women. If one is concerned about the rights of women then stop murdering them, woman-up and respect the choice of that baby to continue to breathe and to live.

The murder of millions of America's babies far outreaches the murder of those babies sacrificed to Baael in ancient Israel, and it is all "justified" with the use of a name for those victims. We are taught by liberals to never call them babies, but to always call them "fetuses," thereby depriving them of the honor and nobility we assign to all human beings. We seem to be constantly trying to extend the term for calling those tiny ones fetuses, even past their actual birth. The most hideous and unconscionable act in the repertoire for aborting babies is to take a born, kicking and crying baby and to kill-abort it. If that is allowed to become a common practice, then when do we stop calling the human being a fetus and recognize the child as a legitimate member of the human race? Does a fetus become a person after five minutes, an hour, a day, a week or maybe twelve years? The real question is how long are we justified in murdering children? This sounds ridiculous I admit, but I do not recognize it as any more ridiculous than to have a Physician take a moving and crying baby into his hands and "abort" that tiny defenseless person, that beautiful child of God, with life and a lifespan ahead of him or her.

The ancients killed their babies in sacrifice to statues they called Baael. We kill our own today for the god of convenience. The ancients had babies they wanted to kill because they thought of them as inconvenient just because they had participated in those sex orgies, just as everyone else was doing. Modern women murder their own because those little people are so very inconvenient, and what is the use in dating if you can't have sex? What's the big deal? Everyone is doing it, so it can't be wrong? Chill out, and leave me alone to have a little fun in life!

HOMOSEXUALITY

There are two very distinct and very different faces of homosexuality; the face of a kind, clever and loveable population such as we all see everywhere we look, on TV, in the News and all over our TVs, and the real-deal face of homosexuality such as we find in Romans 1. It all comes down to a question for you; where do you find your truth, in TV Sitcoms or in the Lord's own book of instruction, The Bible?

I love people, all people, even people who hate me. I work hard to love even the hateful citizens of Planet Earth because I am commanded by God to do exactly that. I love heterosexuals, homosexuals and everyone not included in those two major categories. I was involved in an apartment ministry for seven years, and many of the people to whom I ministered were section eight people, doing the best they could with the sometimes limited talents issued them, to navigate the sea of life. Some of those people were blatant homosexuals, and I loved them up close and personal. I watched two men die of Aids, men I loved. I drove those men around Fort Worth, taking them shopping, to their medical appointments sharing lunches with them and getting to know them.

I recently watched a debate of gubernatorial candidates from Idaho. One older man explained his understanding of homosexuality by reading Romans 1:24-32. Those verses present a personality and a behavioral profile of homosexuals that is far more accurate than the very public image of homosexuals, which they have manufactured and presented to America. I agree with the old politician from Idaho; the Book Of Romans says all that needs to be said on the subject of homosexuality. Romans 1 instructs us in the truth, "Wherefore God also gave them up to uncleanness through the lusts of their own hearts, to dishonor their own bodies between themselves: Who changed the truth of God into a lie, and worshipped and served the creature more than the creator, who is blessed forever. Amen. For this cause God gave them up unto vile affections: for even their women did change the natural use unto that which is against nature. And likewise also the men, leaving the natural use of the woman, burned in their lust one toward another, men with men working that which is unseemly, and receiving in themselves that recompense of their error which was meet. And even as they did not like to retain God in their knowledge, God gave them over to a reprobate mind, to do those things which are not convenient. Being filled with all unrighteousness, fornication, wickedness, covetousness, maliciousness, full of envy, murder, debate, deceit, malignity, whisperers, backbiters, haters of God, despiteful, proud, boasters, inventors of evil things, disobedient to parents, without understanding, covenant-breakers, without natural affection, implacable, unmerciful, who knowing the judgment of God, that they which commit such things are worthy of death, not only do the same but take pleasure in them that do them."

In 2009 I wrote and published a Book on Homosexuality in America, based in the most part on things a former Homosexual, Rusty Walker, had told me about how he escaped the "lifestyle, " through Scripture reading and unceasing prayer. The Title of that Book: THE LAVENDER LIE; The Great Homosexual Deception of America. That deception was so cleverly planned and smoothly executed by the so-called main-stream media who were apparently in on the lie from its inception. The lie had two main features; that at least 10% of Americans were part of a movement growing like wildfire, of living as homosexuals, and that because homosexuals were "born that way", their condition was a natural act of God's, and it was irreversible. For homosexuality to survive and grow those two lies had to be somehow hammered into the consciousness of what appeared to be the great majority of Americans.

This lengthy excerpt from Rusty's book is necessary for anyone to understand how these lies were packaged and presented in what is probably the greatest Public Relations Hoax since Hitler convinced

Germans that all Jews were wicked and needed to be exterminated. The following is written from the viewpoint of a homosexual activist, boastfully telling you what he and his friends have accomplished.

"In 1973 we scored a major triumph by persuading the American Psychiatric Association to stop including homosexuality on their list of mental disorders. We achieved that victory through intimidation and help from those of us who were on the inside, practicing Medicine.

Then came Aids. They began by calling the disease GRID or Gay Related Immunodeficiency Disease. We pressured the establishment to change the name of the disease to AIDS, Acquired Immune Deficiency Syndrome. It was 1978 when the study, by Alan P. Bell and Martin S. Wineberg, was released, citing that 43% of homosexuals had more than 500 partners during their lifetimes. When AIDS was introduced to the notorious bath houses of San Francisco, we had an almost instant epidemic. In the very early days of the AIDS Epidemic, nothing seemed good for our movement. Straight America looked at the whole ugly spectacle, and pronounced that it was what we deserved. God was destroying us, and that might not be a bad thing at all, thought many straight Americans.

Then something happened that turned the tide of public opinion. The first highly visible one of us to die from AIDS was Rock Hudson, in 1985. Then, in 1988 ABC News anchor, Max Robinson died of AIDS followed by ballet superstar Rudolf Nureyev in 1993. These were all people who Americans knew and loved.

The sympathy factor began to loom large in how people perceived not only AIDS, but all of us. We began to move ever so slowly from being hated for bringing the epidemic to America, to being perceived as the victims of this terrible plague.

I was diagnosed as HIV Positive in 1992. I sadly report today that everyone of those men who was diagnosed with me is dead today. God kept me alive for some reason, and I believe I am fulfilling that reason as I write these words. (Rusty Walker's words.)

There were groups of us who really hurt our cause, and all that we were trying to do. One such group was a group called ACT UP, the AIDS Coalition to Unleash Power. One action that hurt our image occurred on December 10, 1989. A group of homosexuals stormed Saint Patrick's Cathedral during a Mass, shouting and throwing consecrated hosts on the floor. Many of the demonstrators were members of ACT UP and they carried signs proclaiming, "Keep your church out of my crotch," "Keep your rosaries off my ovaries," and "Eternal life to Cardinal John O'Conner, now."

What was needed for us, was clearly direction and a touch of sophistication. We found that in February 1988 when we gathered for a War Council. They came, 175 of the leaders of the movement from across the country, to Warrenton, Virginia. Out of that meeting came a document that has to be considered a brilliant operational plan. The document was titled AFTER THE BALL; How America Will Conquer its Fear and Hatred of Gays in America in the 1990's, by Marshall Kirk and Hunter Madsen. Both men were Harvard graduates. Kirk was a researcher in neuropsychiatry, and he designed aptitude tests for people with IQ Scores over 200. Madsen, with a Ph.D. in politics, brought cutting edge knowledge from his field of study, public persuasion tactics and social marketing.

Their work set in motion a 3-step program to perpetuate the great lie that homosexuality is a good thing, and that homosexuals deserve special consideration regarding the protection of their perversion, and the granting of special rights and privileges to members of their group. The three steps are "desensitization", "jamming" and "conversion".

"Desensitization" is the flooding of the senses with messages and minutiae about the good old boys who call themselves gay. When the people have seen and heard so much about the Good News of Homosexuality, they become tired, exhausted with the message, and accept it as a fact they no longer need to hear or see. As soon as Americans decide, "Okay, so that is what being gay is. So what!" we have already won. The people don't have to buy the tee shirts and drink the Kool-Aid. The battle is won, not when the people accept the message, but when they become so bored with it that they ignore it. That is victory.

"Jamming" is taking one side of a story, and hammering it into the consciousness of the citizenry so hard and so long that they buy off on it. One example of a "jamming" campaign that worked well, was the media blitz we used following the 1988 murder of University of Wyoming Freshman, Matthew Shepard. The two men who beat him to death were essentially ignored, while we used a media friendly blitz to blame the Christian Right. Focus On the Family, among other Christian groups, had run ads aimed at homosexuals, simply stating that for members of the homosexual community who wanted out, they were willing to help. We managed to jam the media with our complaints that the murder had occurred because the Christian Right had created an atmosphere of gay bashing and hatred.

One of our biggest breaks in that campaign came from Katie Couric, who, on the Today Show, asked Wyoming Governor Jim Geringer, "Some gay rights activists have said that some conservative political organizations like the Christian Coalition, the Family Research Council and Focus on the Family are contributing to this anti-homosexual atmosphere by having an ad campaign saying if you are a homosexual you can change your orientation. That prompts people to say, 'If I meet someone who's homosexual I'm going to try to take action to try to convince them, or try to harm them.' Do you believe that such groups are contributing to this climate?"

Do you want to know how ridiculous the charges were that the Christian Right caused the death of Matthew Shepard? In 2004 ABC News 20/20 opened a vigorous new investigation of the crime, and concluded that homosexuality very likely was not even a factor in the murder, and that Matthew Shepard had been murdered for his money. The truth did almost nothing to erase the effects of the lie. America was already satisfied that the Christian Right had orchestrated a Nation-Wide environment of hatred for homosexuals, and was as guilty for Matthew Shepard's Death as they would have been if they had beaten him to death. The rebuttal on the 20/20 Program was sort of like telling a jury to disregard what they had just heard.

Please understand this; the homosexual front that you see portrayed by the media is not the real picture of what homosexuality is. You will never hear, for example, that most serial killers and child molesters were homosexuals first. Go to any Gay Pride Parade and you will see men carrying huge banners for the NAMBLA Organization. NAMBLA stand for the North American Man-Boy Love Association.

Former FBI Agent Bob Hamer is the man who infiltrated NAMBLA. Here is a transcript of things he said on October 8, 2009, in an interview with Sean Hannity on FOX News.

"The infiltration was fairly easy, they had a website, I paid $35, I joined the group, They sent me a letter, praising me for my courageous step in joining the organization. I began to get emails from them - I was subscribed to their magazine, they started to send me their magazine, but they wouldn't allow me to attend any of their secret underground meetings until I'd been a member for three years, and had been sponsored by another active duty member.

They're hiding behind the First Amendment, ostensibly they claim that they are designed to abolish age-of-consent laws. I was in the organization for three years, I attended two of their national conferences, I spoke with many of their members, I corresponded with about 175 of their members. At no time during my three-year infiltration was there ever any discussion about modifying age-of-consent laws, abolishing age-of-consent laws. Every conversation I had was about where to go to have sex with little boys - how they could attract little boys, how they could groom little boys: that was their agenda.

At one of the conferences I attended, there was a discussion about, that it was actually ok, proper, there was nothing wrong with having oral sex on an eighteen-month-old boy, the rationale being that little boys play with themselves, they enjoy touching themselves, so the men were actually bringing pleasure to the little boys by committing oral sex."

I am not saying in any way that all homosexuals are pedophiles, What I am certain of is that many pedophiles, to include Jeffery Dahmer and John Wayne Gacy, were homosexuals before they became pedophiles. There are a plethora of studies on whether or not homosexuality and pedophilia are related. The findings are all over the place, and some of those alleged "scientific" studies are not even close to scientific! One group, for example doesn't relate child molestation of little boys and little girls to homosexual acts. I am indeed saying that supporting so-called Gay Rights is opening the door for the acceptance of pedophilia, bestiality, and all other perversions. As soon as the door of public acceptance has been opened, then the pedophiles and all others will rush in with the crowd, and they too will be demanding their "rights."

The third and most crucial step in the public brainwashing process is "conversion". After the public has been thoroughly "desensitized" and "jammed", they are ready to be converted to thinking as we think, for supporting our "rights," to include the right to be married. "Conversion" works because of the need of so many individuals to be politically correct, with the people who are "in." Many Americans are far more concerned with being in conformance than they are about being right, and that is why "conversion" is working. Americans are becoming pro-gay because they have been led to believe that everyone else, who is anybody, is on-board.

Where does it all end? It does indeed have a logical (at least to us) conclusion. It ends when society has bought off on us, and our rights to live without criticism. That has already happened in Canada where a broadcaster who has the audacity to use scripture to support his assumption that homosexuality is wrong, will be prosecuted. We want opposition to our cause silenced, and we will not stop until the law supports our "right" to live without criticism. Believe it, because it will happen. Your freedom of speech will simply be redefined as a "hate crime" anytime you stray from the party line of political correctness." 2. I believe that I would be imprisoned a few years from now, for having written these words back in 2009.

After reading what the homosexuals of America planned, there is only one conclusion regarding their effectiveness; they have accomplished their goals with stunning results and far-reaching conversion of most Americans to virtually all of their propaganda, including the lie that they represent ten per cent of our population. The lie regarding their population was launched with the publication of Sexual Behavior in The Human Male in 1948 and Sexual Behavior in the Human Female in 1953, by a zoologist, Dr. Alfred Kinsey. Dr. Kinsey is the best example I can think of, of what has been called "The Experimenter Effect," the fact that experimenters (Data gatherers, analysts and publishers) tend to report results they believed to be true before they began their experiments. Dr. Kinsey was a perverted sexual creature sometimes requiring bizarre sexual practices from his employees and fellow researchers. Dr. Judith Reisman, has been the leading critic of Kinsey's work. Kinsey claimed that infant boys wanted and needed sexual stimulation, setting off a firestorm of reactions from the very twisted international pedophile community, standing by to abuse baby boys. Dr. Reisman estimates that as many as 2035 documented cases of infant abuse were attributable to the Kinsey report, sexual Behavior in the Human Male. 3.

Kinsey's work was obviously flawed by the fact that many of the men he interviewed came from Penitentiaries where, of course, homosexual activities dominate, and even from members of homosexual groups. If Kinsey had submitted his "research" in a reputable graduate school, he would have been required to take remedial training to learn the meaning of unbiased research. Amazingly, both homosexuals and homosexual friendly reporters continue to use Kinsey's bogus projection that 10% of American males are homosexuals. 4 Liberal leaning media and organizations such as The Washington Times and the American Psychological Association cling tenaciously to the obviously bogus 10% estimate. 5.

Most researchers, operating free of any obvious and apparent homosexual bias, report that the actual number of exclusively homosexual men in America runs from 1.7 % to 3 %. A recent Government Report found 2.3% of Americans gay or bisexual. 6.

We could examine figures forever on the percentage of homosexuals in America, and the one constant would be that the numbers would almost always run from 1.3% to 10% with the higher numbers almost always coming from sources with a homosexual agenda to promote. Based on the hundreds of figures I have seen during the past two days I think it is safe to say that about 3% or less of Americans are exclusively homosexual. That is not nearly as relevant and as important as the fact that most Americans believe that homosexuals make up from 10% to as high as 40% of our population.

The fact that the President of these United States displayed more positive emotion at the Democratic Convention when it was announced that the Democrats had made great strides in promoting the

Homosexual Agenda, and in particular, the legalization of same-sex marriage than at any other time. Cameras behind the President clearly showed him dancing when pro-homosexual statements were made. Add Pharaoh Obama I's demonstrated delight at promotion of the homosexual agenda, to the fact that he seems overjoyed to welcome other homosexuals aboard by telephone calls to anyone, athlete or celebrity, who announces that (s)he is practicing homosexual behavior. On July 15, 2014 The Cover of Newsweek Magazine featured a photo of Pharaoh Obama I beneath a rainbow colored halo, along with the bold headline, OBAMA, FIRST GAY PRESIDENT. 7. There was no fiery response from Washington, and I personally believe, based on nothing but what I know about Pharaoh Obama I, that Obama saw the copy before it was published, and that he approved of it.

This paragraph is not validated any place I know by anyone I know, but I believe it will happen. I believe that Pharaoh Obama I no longer cares what you, or anyone, or everyone thinks about him. I also believe that he is an activist for whatever cause he is currently wrapping his mind and his heart around. Right now the primary cause in Mr. Obama's life is the promotion of homosexuality in America. I predict that within the next two years Pharaoh Obama I will come out of the closet and make the biggest and most spectacular appeal for the Homosexual cause that has ever been made. Again, this is not prophecy, but simply my prediction based on all I have seen and learned about Pharaoh Obama I.

WE CAN'T CHANGE BECAUSE WE WERE BORN THIS WAY

Homosexuals and their advocates often compare their sexual behavior to race. They say that like black men, they were born that way-homosexuals. If I were a Black man, hearing that nonsense would cause great rolling clouds of steam to emanate from my ears and nostrils. Blackness is part of the human formula for who a man is, what he was born to be and will be until he sucks in his last delicious breath of air.

If I wanted to prove that sexual preference is not attached or included in the makeup of a man at birth all I would need to do is to place a lone black male, and a lone white homosexual on separate and equal desert islands and leave them there for life. The black man would live and die black because that is what he is, what God gave him as a part of his identity at birth. The homosexual male, on the other hand, would cease being a homosexual the instant all other males were removed from his accessibility. He would never again practice a homosexual act, and therefore he would never again be a homosexual. Here is the truth and the difference between sexual preference and race. Race is part of who you are, sexual orientation is part of what you do. Race is inherent and unchangeable. Sexual orientation is a choice and can be changed by simply abstaining from the behavior.

The great lie of homosexuality is that it is inherent and unchangeable. That lie perpetuates homosexuality, attempting to desensitize people by forcing them to hear the lie so often that they convert to believing it.

I have a source I will not name here who has attended high level strategy meetings in the National Homsexual Community. My source told me that the homosexuals will announce soon that Homosexuality is actually a choice and that it has been all along, as they clamored for recognition of homosexuality bestowed on people at birth. When they finally admit the truth that each of them chooses homosexuality then they can say, "So what! We're gay and you can't do anything about that."

HOW TO REALLY LOVE A HOMOSEXUAL

One of the most loving things I can do for a homosexual is to tell them that their sin just might send them to the torments of Hell for eternity. One thing I cannot stand, with regard to homosexuality, is to see what they do, and believe that no person has ever explained the eternal consequences of their behavior.

Homosexual sin is, like all sins, except blasphemy of the Holy Ghost, a forgivable affront against God. Living a homosexual lifestyle is different, because when sin is flaunted and glorified by the sinner it becomes a massive affront against God, insults God and His commandments, and can result in condemnation to Hell for eternity. God forgives any sin, but it is doubtful that He will be able to overlook a sin which has become an identity for the sinner and a cause the sinner passionately espouses.

THE IMPORTANCE OF AMERICA'S TREATMENT OF ISRAEL

The standard for the International treatment of Israel for every person and every Nation on earth was established thousands of years ago when God spoke to Abraham, the Father of Israel, and He said, as recorded in Genesis 12:2-3:

"And I will make of thee a great Nation, and I will bless thee, and make thy name great; and thou shalt be a blessing, And I will bless them that bless thee, and

curse them that curseth thee: and in thee shall all the families of the earth be blessed."

A wise statesman will read and understand the implications of those small verses, and will design his Nation's relationship with Israel based on what God promised Abraham. These words are given strong emphasis when they are read with this verse from Obadiah 1:15, "For the day of the Lord is near upon all the heathen: as thou has done unto (Israel) it shall be done unto thee: thy reward shall return upon thine own head."

In 580 BC Nebuchadnezzar took the entire population of Israel into slavery and marched those he spared out of Israel. Usually when an entire population is forcibly removed from their homeland, they cease to exist as a Nation. The people of Israel were kept in bondage for a full 70 years and then they returned home, built a wall around their city and rebuilt their temple.

Amazingly, Israel was again sent into exile for 1878 years, they remained scattered around the world until, on May 14, 1948, Israel become a Nation once again, claiming the Ancient Land Of Israel which had been given by God to Abraham. They returned home, and are still coming home today, maintaining their own Religion and their own Hebrew Language.

The Land of Israel, the real estate itself, was given to Israel by God. When America sides with the enemies of Israel and attempts to trade in a so-called "land for peace" arrangement they are breaking the ancient curse in Geneses and attempting to take away part of Israel, which is non-negotiable real estate, deeded by God to Abraham and to his descendants. Of the dozens of violations of human rights and

Constitutional freedoms committed by Pharaoh Obama I, and his associates, violating the Ancient Covenant God made with Israel, is the most upsetting to anyone who understands the meaning of the Abrahamic Covenant. 8

IMPORTANT POINTS IN THIS CHAPTER

1.   Abortion is the killing of babies because they pose an inconvenience to the parents

2.   Half of all babies aborted are female, therefore nullifying the argument that abortion is an issue of woman's rights.

3.   Romans 1 presents a profile of homosexuals, very different from the profile manufactured for sit-coms on TV

4.   Homosexual acts, when performed without the action of being made into a lifestyle or a cause, are forgivable sins.

5.   Although Americans believe that 10% of Americans are homosexuals, the truth is that homosexuals comprise only 3% or less of the American population.

CHAPTER SEVEN

THE NINEVEH EFFECT IN AMERICA

The Book of Jonah is only a few pages in length and it tells a story of a Kingdom, Nineveh, that, because of their very sinful behavior had caused God to decide to destroy the city. The destruction God planned for Nineveh was probably much like the destruction he had previously demonstrated by reigning fire and brimstone from Heaven on Sodom and Gomorrah. Imagine that wrath of God pouring down from the sky and virtually destroying great cities.

God chose a man named Jonah to go to Nineveh and tell the people of that city what he planned to do to them and to Nineveh. Jonah hated the city and probably the people of Nineveh, and probably thought they were so wicked that they weren't even worth saving. Instead of heading for Nineveh, as God had commanded him to do, he fled, booking passage on a boat, as if he could outrun God. Jonah was correctly identified by the crew on the boat as the cause for a violent storm that threatened to sink the boat. At his request, the crew threw Jonah overboard. Jonah was then swallowed by a great whale and had three days in the belly of that whale to think things over in his relationship with God. When the whale vomited him up on the shore, God was waiting to tell Jonah to continue on his journey and go to warn the Ninevites of the wrath of God to come.

Nineveh was a great city and it took three days to merely walk across the city. Jonah was a day's journey into the city before God gave him the words to say to the citizens of Nineveh. He was instructed to tell them that in forty days God was going to destroy Nineveh. The people knew from oral and written histories what had happened at Sodom and Gomorrah, so they were afraid and listened respectfully to the warning Jonah was giving them.

Historians speculate that the digestive enzymes in the belly of that whale had probably bleached Jonah's skin, every hair on his body and his clothes. He was probably a strange sight, snow white and walking through the streets of Nineveh shouting his warning. He probably also spoke with the power of the Holy Ghost, causing the people to listen to his words and to believe his warning with all of their hearts. The Bible tells us that in response to Jonah's message, "So the people of Nineveh believed God, and proclaimed a fast, and put on sackcloth, from the greatest of them even to the least of them." When the King saw what the people were doing he made the fast an official event, "and he caused it to be proclaimed and published through Nineveh by the decree of the King and his nobles,..." Notice the repenting of Nineveh came originally from the people, and then the King lent his authority to what was already happening. Then in Chapter 3:10, we read an unusual verse, as God changes His intentions, "And God saw their works, that they turned from their evil way; and God repented of the evil, that He had said that He would do unto them; and He did it not."

Now I want you to imagine a modern day Jonah and a modern day Nineveh type incident. Our modern Jonah lives in Portland, Oregon, and God appears to Him and instructs him to go to Hollywood, and to tell those sinful people that He plans to destroy them in only one month. Jonah wants no part of that assignment so he heads for Canada. God turns him around and gets him all the way down the Coast to Hollywood.

What I am now going to describe, you will only understand if you fully appreciate that God can do all things. For God to do what I will now describe could only happen if some, a lot of them, God's favorite people had been praying hard for the people in Hollywood, which is not really known as a bastion of Christianity. Imagine, for just a few seconds, that God moved mightily in Hollywood and people had the scales removed from their eyes, and the plugs taken out of their ears and they really heard Jonah and they were influenced by God to hear and accept his message.

As Jonah walked and talked, God amplified his voice, adding the use of heavenly woofers and tweeters, so that his words rolled from his lips, in a low rumbling thunder sort of a baritone, and he could be heard for over a mile from wherever he stood. The people heard, they understood and across the city people fell to their knees, and they asked God to forgive them.

Across the great city hundreds of moving vans pulled up in front of Condos and homes, and men and women who had been living with unmarried partners, moved out. They carried their belongings, loaded vans and drove away from their sins. As they worked and as they drove away they sang a song most of them didn't even know that they knew. Their voices rose up as a great choir, as they sang, HOW GREAT THOU ART."

Workers could been seen hauling great loads of DVDs out of the Pornography studios and throwing them into dumpsters. Inside those studios, handsome men and beautiful women, who had starred in hundreds of Pornographic Movies stood before cameras, and spoke with authority on how they had been rescued by Jesus Christ and what a wonderful thing it was to serve Him.

Liquor store owners and drug dealers poured their inventory into gutters and watched as it was washed away into the sewers of the city. Children who had been living as prostitutes on the sidewalks of Hollywood hurried to bus stations to return home to their parents, who they suddenly began to love more than they ever believed they could love anyone. Children who did not have bus fare were given money by their pimps, and by police officers.

Criminals walked into police stations and turned themselves in, admitting their crimes and asking forgiveness. A few hours after he began to speak, Jonah was taken to the Hollywood bowl where he told thousands of listeners about salvation and about the mercy of God. Before dark, he was standing on the fifty yard line at the Los Angeles Coliseum.

He continued to speak without any microphones or speakers, and as the crowd grew, so did the volume of his words. Over a hundred thousand knelt, held hands and prayed the sinner's prayer, begging for forgiveness.

Outrageous? Unbelievable? Citizens, God alone can straighten out this great mess we have made of this Country He gave us. No candidate can fix this mess. God alone can restore and redeem America. You and I can make that happen. Go ahead and join me. Just ask God to have mercy on us all. See what happens. You are going to be surprised and very possibly blessed in an abundance you have never even imagined. Go ahead. Try it and watch what happens.

CHAPTER EIGHT

PRESIDENT REAGAN'S FAVORITE VERSE

"If we ever forget that we are a Nation under God, then we will be a Nation gone under."
-President Ronald Reagan

THE SINGLE BIBLE VERSE THAT CAN STILL SAVE AMERICA

On January 20, 1981, Ronald Reagan laid his hand on a verse in his mother's Bible, II Chronicles 7:14, and took the oath of office as President of The United States. President Eisenhower had chosen the same verse to touch as he took his oath of office. By Noon it was 55 degrees, the warmest day ever for a Presidential Inauguration. The words to the oath the president was touching are these, "If my people, who are called by my name, will humble themselves, seek my face, pray, and turn from their wicked ways, I will hear from heaven, I will forgive their sins, and heal their land." The rest of this brief chapter will examine those words closely and help all who would listen, to know that America can still be saved.

"IF..." That tiny, two-letter word signifies that the author, God Himself, is about to offer you the reader, a contract. The verse specifies that if you will do four things, (which you should be doing anyway), God will take notice and do two very amazing things, only He can do.

"...my People, who are called by my name." That narrows the people being addressed by these words to you, a Christian, and other believers, and alerts you that these instructions are for God's People, and that you do not have to worry about getting sinners to heed these instructions. Take care of yourself and other believers, and God will do the rest."

"...will humble themselves, ..." Jesus was said to be "no respecter of persons." He did not care what you rode, ate, wore or where you lived. To Jesus there was no distinction between common men, such as He chose to follow him, and learned men of great wealth and power. He told his apostles to go out and win souls, wearing what they had on their backs. He said of Himself, "Foxes have their dens, the birds of the air have their nests, but the son of man hath no place to lay his head." Luke 9:58. I recently taught a 7 lesson video coarse for our Seminary on evangelism with emphasis on street preaching, and one of my lectures was "Come down off your high horse, come down to earth and love God's people." That is what I suggest that you do if you are ready to comply with God's command that you "Humble yourself..."

"...seek my face.." Imagine, the Son of God telling you to "Seek my face." Touching someone's face is an act of profound intimacy unless you are a barber, a plastic surgeon, or a dentist. God Himself is encouraging each of us to become His lover, and to seek His precious face.

"...Pray..." there it is, in four letters, the formula for getting as close to your loving Savior as you possibly can. Paul wrote in a word, when and how to pray and the word was, "unceasingly." I see people every day with cell phone devices stuck in their ears, having conversations over things so trivial that I am so glad I do not have to listen in on those conversations. My advice is to ditch the cell phone, just stop all of this texting nonsense, and take God with you instead of those things you stick in your ears. Talk to him about the traffic on your commute and about the help you need in cleaning up your language. Talk to Him about your children, your marriage and your salvation, and if you feel like it, talk to Him about where to get a good haircut. Just talk to Him as you would if he were sitting next to you in your car. God does not want to hear you recite someone else's words, but He is attentive to you and your very own thoughts. In Matthew 6:6, "But thou, when thou prayest, enter into thy closet, and when thou hast shut the door, pray to the Father which is in secret, and the Father which seeth in secret, shall reward thee openly."

"...and turn from their wicked ways..." God never allows you to be tempted beyond your ability to resist. I Corinthians 10:13, "There hath no temptation taken you but such as is common to man: but God is faithful, who will not suffer you to be tempted above that you are able, but will with the temptation also make a way to escape, that ye may be able to bear it." Think of sin as spiritual Kryptonite. Just as prayer connects man to God, sin separates him from God. When Jesus told people (Twice) to go and sin no more, He certainly knew that no man is capable of living completely without sin. However, through our prayerful connection to God we can fight the good fight to resist temptation. It took me years and many failures to win my battle over alcohol addiction, but through God's help, I haven't had a drink in 26 years. It helps me to always remember, in regard to sins and temptations, Philippians 4:13, "I can do all things through Christ which strengtheneth me."

"...and I will hear from Heaven..." Never forget Who is communicating this contract to you. This is God Himself saying, I will hear and I will listen to the prayers of my people. Thus far God has told you that His people must do four things. Good people do these things as a matter of daily routines, so God is asking for you to reach out to His people who do not necessarily live righteously. The exciting part of this message follows, as God tells you the two things He is prepared to do.

" ...And I will forgive their sins..." Sins are offences

against God and His word, so none other could possibly forgive sins. The significance here is that God is telling you (everything God says He will do is a covenant). I like what I heard Ed Young, Junior, say about a covenant, when he called it a "contract on steroids". God says it and that is the only thing you ever heard that you can count on 1000%. Men make promises and sign contracts and they break them so often that we need judges and lawyers to make sense of it all. If God says it will happen, then it is true and you can believe it with all of your being. When God forgives sins He forgets them and they never happened as far as He is concerned. That is divine forgiveness.

"...and I will heal their land..." How would you like to live in an America with no abortion, with no political correctness standing in opposition to so many of God's own commandments? God can make all of that sin and silliness go away or back to Hell where I suspect much of it originated? God can heal our land and if you really believed that, you would probably never stop praying. Please spend the rest of this day thinking about what God has promised to do, "Forgive their sins and heal their land." Instead of talking about some lame movie or sports, tell a friend about what God has promised His people, and ask your friend if he understands that promise. Try it. You might be surprised.

CHAPTER NINE

WOULD GOD REALLY PERFORM THOSE
MIRACLES? EVEN NOW?

"Don't give up before the miracle happens."
– Fannie Flagg

*"Miracles seldom occur in the lives of those who do
not consider them possible."* **-Neale Donald Walsch**

DEAR GOD, PLEASE, JUST ONE MORE TIME?

So, here we are, you and me, praying. You feel an electric rush of faith, a reverberation from every cell in your body. You believe and so do I. So we pray, "God, please, just one more time, God, bless America."

Then the sound of many rushing waters fills the world, as God responds, "What? Again? I've done that so many times, and look at how you still behave. Why should I bless America again?"

Do not miss the great miracle happening in this account. The greatest miracle is our Faith, and we only have that because of the endless Grace and Mercy of God. We believe and we believe because God caused us to have the faith required to see what has not yet happened, and even what certainly should not, in an ordered world, happen. Hebrews 11:1, communicates, "Faith is the evidence of things hoped for, the evidence of things not seen."

Let me give you just a little assistance as you work to accumulate your own faith. Consider just a few of the things God has done, already, to bless America.

In November of 1746, on a beautiful, sunny day, the citizens of Boston were startled to look out into their harbor and see a great armada of French ships, carrying a normal compliment of heavy cannon and about 12,000 French Troops. The Bostonians knew exactly why the French were in their harbor. They were about to launch a massive attack, and destroy the people of Boston and their city. Their orders were to begin by wiping out Boston, and then to proceed down the coast of America wiping out the cities along the Eastern Seaboard, and then to continue into the West Indies with their raids, killing and destroying all who might resist a coming French Invasion.

Because of the beautiful weather the people of Boston, walked briskly on their way to an assembly at the Old South Meeting House in South Boston. When they arrived the Reverend Thomas Prince mounted the tall pulpit and prayed this prayer.

"Deliver us from the enemy!" the minister implored. "Send thy tempest, Lord, upon the waters to the eastward! Raise Thy right hand. Scatter the ships of our tormentors and drive them hence. Sink their proud frigates beneath the power of Thy winds." 1.

What happened next was almost in perfect synchronization with the prayer. Dark black clods rolled over Boston and out into the harbor. With the clouds, God delivered a heavy, hammering rain and tumultuous winds. The majority of the French ships sank in the harbor, and all but a thousand troops were drowned that morning. Legend holds that even though no man was in the bell tower, the great bells rang out and could be heard by the French, out in the harbor. The people prayed and the enemy was destroyed in a matter of minutes!

In another instance, the formidable British Army, which included 400 warships and over 32,000 men, armed and well trained and disciplined in the arts of war, was camped within rifle range of General Washington and his troops of the United States Continental Army. The Americans and the British waited for the dawn so the final annihilation of the Americans could begin.

Certainly throughout the American encampment, men prayed through the night, and as the sun begin to rise, Washington and his men saw God's answer to their prayers. A mysterious fog bank was floating just above the water and into a perfect position to cover the escape of the Continental Army. Washington's men went silently to their oars and rowed across the East River in New York, completely covered from the peering eyes of the British. 2. As soon as the Americans had passed directly in front of the British, and were safe on the far shore of the river, the cloud of fog dissolved, as mysteriously as it had appeared. The British were astonished, because the American Army had very mysteriously disappeared.

On July 9, 1155, George Washington was fighting in the French and Indian war. He fought with a small American unit, assigned to the British Army. The unit was marching out of a fort, in a heavily wooded area near Pittsburgh, when they were suddenly ambushed. The British-American troops responded exactly as they had learned from fighting on the Continent in Europe. They lined up shoulder to shoulder and returned fire to a force of French and Indian soldiers firing at them from cover behind rocks and trees, from the tops of trees, and from beneath fallen trees. At the end of two hours 713 of the British-American unit of 1300 had been killed, while only 30 of the French and Indian Force had been shot.

Washington and the survivors retreated back to Fort Cumberland in Maryland, arriving there on July 17, 1755. The next day Washington wrote a letter to his family, explaining that when he took off his coat after the battle he found four bullet holes in the coat, and any one of them would have been fatal, but he was untouched. In his letter he wrote that... "By the all-powerful dispensations of Providence, I have been protected beyond all human probability or expectation. 3. Fifteen years later, after hostilities from the French-Indian wars had ended, Washington met with an old Indian Chief, who had traveled a long distance to speak with him. The Indian told Washington that he, himself, had fired at George Washington 17 times during that battle of so many years ago. The Indian then said, "When I realized you were protected by your God I spread the word among our men to not fire at you, because God was protecting you."

Consider this small sampling of reports of God's direct intervention saving battles and keeping America and our Nation alive. I believe that these few accounts and many others are true, and if they are true, then each occurrence is sterling proof that God still can and will save America, when God's people pray for America. Say these three words with me now, and believe with all of your heart that it can happen, "God Bless America."

FOOTNOTES

CHAPTER ONE

1. http://cgi.cnn.com/allpolitics/1996/news/9603
/o3keyes/article filed on March 3, 1996, titled,
Minutes Before Debate GOP Contender, Alan
Keyes, Taken Into Custody

2. http://en.wikipedia.org/wiki/alan_keyes

3. http://www.cowboy.lyrics.com/tabs/mcclintock
-harry/big-rock-candy-mountain-
3883.htmlhttp://www.theconservativetreehouse
.com2014/15/peggy-joseph-

4. http://www.cnsnews.com/news/article/first-
term-obama-increased-debt-50521-household-
more-first-42-presidents-53-terms, Article by
Terence P. Jeffery, RSS, filed January 19, 2013

5. http://wws.huffingtonpost.com/2012/10/08/mitt-romney-liar-obama-campaign-n-1949732.html

CHAPTER TWO

1.   http://amzn.to/SJBzEv Marilyn Monroe sings Happy Birthday To J.F Kennedy.

2.http://endoftheamericandream.com/archives/why-are-dozens-of-high-ranking-officers-being-purged-from-the-u-s-military

3.www.washingtonpost.com/blogs/post-partisan/wp/2013/10/23/why-lies-about-obama-resist-the truth, article by Jonathan Capehart, Oct 23, 2013

4.www.mediate.com/tv/:mclaughlin-guest-ambassador-stevens-wasn't-murdered, report posted by Evan McMurry, May 11,2014

5.http://www.mediaite.com/online/rep-steve-king-wants-to-make-ambassador-stevens-autopsy-report-public/

6. Reuters, Feb 26, 2014, 6:16 am

http://www.nytimes.com/2012/05/18/us/florida-attempts-to-scrub-illegal-voters.html?_r=0

CHAPTER THREE

1.   http://amzn.to/SJBzEv Marilyn Monroe sings Happy Birthday To J.F Kennedy.

2.http://endoftheamericandream.com/archives/why-are-dovens-of-high-ranking-officers-being-purged-from-the-u-s-military

3.www.washingtonpost.com/blogs/post-partisan/wp/2013/10/23/why-lies-about-obama-resist-the truth, article by Jonathan Capehart, Oct 23, 2013

4.www.mediate.com/tv/:mclaughlin-guest-ambassador-stevens-wasn't-murdered, report posted by Evan McMurry, May 11,2014

5.http://www.mediaite.com/online/rep-steve-king-wants-to-make-ambassador-stevens-autopsy-report-public/

6. Reuters, Feb 26, 2014, 6:16 am

7. http://www.nytimes.com/2012/05/18/us/florida-attempts-to-scrub-illegal-voters.html?_r=0

CHAPTER FOUR

1. http://en.wikipedia.org/wiki/Superconducting_Super_Collider

2. S.E. Cupp, LOSING OUR RELIGION; The Liberal Media's Attack on Christianity, Threshold Editions, 2010.

3. Ann Coulter, GODLESS; The Church of Liberalism, Three Rivers Press, an imprint of Crown Publishing Group, A division of Random House, 2006

4. S.E. Cupp, LOSING OUR RELIGION.

5

http://en.wikipedia.org/wiki/Georg_Wilhelm_Friedrich_Hegel

1. http://freethoughtpedia.com/wiki/Stalin%2C_Mao_Zedong_and_Pol_Pot

2. https://www.youtube.com/watch?v=eUJE9YfsbNQ

3. http://www.actupny.org/reports/elders.html

4. http://www.fox45now.com/shared/news/top-stories/stories/wrgt_vid_21925.shtml

5. http://www.fireandreamitchell.com/rev-wright/god-damn-america-rev-wright/

6. *http://www.huffingtonpost.com/2012/11/27/ja mie-foxx-obama-lord-and-savior-furor-soul-train-awards_n_2199439.html*

7. Starnes, Todd, *GOD LESS AMERICA,* Front Line, Charisma Media, Charisma Book Group.

CHAPTER FIVE

1.http://www.jeremiahproject.com/newworldorder/he gelian-dialectic.html

2. http://rense.com/general11/ksss.htm

3. 3.http://www.rootforamerica.com/webroot/blog /2012/01/23/biggest-rebuke-ever-for-mainstream-media/#sthash.Kb69awL2.dpuf

4. http://www.americanthinker.com/2008/09/bar ack_obama_and_the_strategy.html

CHAPTER SIX

1. http://biblewalk.wordpress.com/2011/04/22/a pr-22/

2. Rusty Walker as told to Marvin Sprouse, THE LAVENDER LIE; The Great Homosexual Deception of America. 2009, Sprouse Publishing

3. http://www.wnd.com/2010/10/213741/k, article in WND, 10/11/2010, by Dr. Judith Reisman, *KINSEY MINIONS CONTINUE CHILD SEX ABUSE*

4. http://www.renewamerica.com/columns/husto n/060314, article by Warner Todd Huston, 10% of Americans are gay; urban myth explored, March 14, 2006

5. http://www.equip.org/articles/what-percentage-of-people-are-homosexuals/

6. http://news.yahoo.com/government-report-finds-2-3-percent-americans-gay-194107587.html;_ylt=A0LEVzih5QlU0DsAkARX NyoA;_ylu=X3oDMTEzMW9ucnBwBHNlYwNzcgR wb3MDNARjb2xvA2JmMQR2dGlkA1ZJUDQ3NF 8x, Reuters report, Government Report Finds

2.3% of Americans gay or bisexual, by Curtis Skinner, July 15, 2014.

7. http://abcnews.go.com/Politics/OTUS/newsweek-cover-obama-gay-president/story?id=16338110

8. John McTernan, *AS AMERICA HAS DONE UNTO ISRAEL, Whitaker House, 2006*

CHAPTER NINE

1.http://www.josephsmithacademy.org/wiki/1746-miracle-at-the-old-south-meeting-hous/

2. Chris Stewart and Ted Stewart, *SEVEN MIRACLES THAT SAVED AMERICA*, An Illustrated History, The Shipley Group, 2012.

3. http://www.garymcleod.org/bullet.h